Access to Phonics

Practical Access Strategies to Teach Children with Complex Needs of All Ages

Copyright © 2023 Ann Sullivan.

All rights reserved.

No part of this book can be reproduced in any form or by written, electronic or mechanical, including photocopying, recording, or by any information retrieval system without written permission in writing by the author, *with the exception of the photocopiable resources in the Appendix*.

Although every precaution has been taken in the preparation of this book, the publisher and author assume no responsibility for errors or omissions. Neither is any liability assumed for damages resulting from the use of information contained herein.

ISBN 9798377519461

To Matthew, Ruth and Tom

With thanks to Kerry Thalia of Discover Inclusion
for her illustrations on the resources

Contents

FOREWARD 1

1. INTRODUCTION 3

2. THE READING LANDSCAPE 4

3. PUPILS WITH COMPLEX PROFILES 15

4. ACCESS FOR PUPILS WITH A PHYSICAL DISABILITY................. 18

5. ACCESS FOR PUPILS WHO ARE PRE- OR NONVERBAL 26

6. ACCESS FOR PUPILS WITH A PHYSICAL DISABILTY WHO ARE NONVERBAL 37

7. ACCESS FOR PUPILS WITH SENSORY NEEDS 43

8. ACCESS FOR PUPILS WITH OTHER NEEDS 44

9. TEACHING BLENDING 47

10. TEACHING SEGMENTING 51

11. LISTENING TO A CHILD READ 53

12. SUMMARY 56

REFERENCES 57

APPENDIX - PHOTCOPIABLE RESOURCES 58

GLOSSARY 89

FOREWARD

Learning to read is one of the most challenging undertakings that a person commits to during their lifetime. Because most of us learn to read over the course of several years while we are still children, we forget the cognitive demands and countless hours of practice involved in becoming a capable, confident reader, not least the initial challenge of learning to recognise words. Nevertheless, it is worth the effort: literacy offers people an entirely different way to communicate with the world and to gain from the accumulated knowledge of humanity.

For some people, the challenge of learning to read is greater than for others. They require specialist support in learning to recognise words and methods that are expertly adapted to their specific needs. I have had the privilege of learning about the complexities of this kind of support from the author of this book, and I am delighted that others can now benefit from her experience and insight on this subject.

Christopher Such

Author of 'The Art and Science of Teaching Primary Reading' SAGE Publications (2021)

1. Introduction

How do you teach children to read if they cannot speak?

How do you know they are reading the words correctly or even reading at all?

How do you teach spelling to children if they cannot write or type words?

How do you teach children to read if they have limits to their attention and focus?

How do you teach children with complex profiles to read and spell?

These are some of the questions that I am frequently asked and, since you are reading this book, these are probably ones that you are also looking to have answered. You are in the right place.

I am mostly asked these questions by teachers and teaching assistants working in specialist schools and settings, but more and more these questions are relevant to those working in mainstream schools. For many reasons, such as parental choice or scarcity of places in specialist provision, mainstream schools are increasingly finding that children with complex profiles are placed in early years classes where, of course, initial reading and spelling instruction begins. This book is for anyone teaching children with complex needs to read and spell, whatever the children's age or school provision.

The book provides simple, yet effective, strategies to enable children with complex needs to access, participate in and respond to phonics activities as part of reading and spelling instruction. As well as describing the strategies and giving examples of their use, supporting resources are provided at the end of the book so that you can photocopy them and get started.

Please note that throughout this booklet the word 'teacher' is used to indicate the person working with the child. This is used as shorthand for *'teacher / teaching assistant / speech and language therapist / parent or carer / other adult'*.

2. The Reading Landscape

Let's think about what it is to be a reader. Reading competency is said to be the fluent reading of text with understanding. That means accessing the narrative, message or information contained within. How do we teach children to achieve this and become confident, fluent and engaged readers?

In mainstream schools in England, phonics has been taught as the foundation of reading since 2007 and the practice is well established. This is not the case for other English-speaking countries across the world, where a variety of approaches are taken to the teaching of reading.

The position is somewhat different for specialist schools and settings in England as until 2021 there was little guidance about how reading should be taught to children in these settings. In the DfE's Reading Framework of 2021[1], which describes best practice in the teaching of reading for all children, pupils with moderate to severe and complex needs were included, giving a strong indication of what reading instruction should look like for them.

This has not come out of nowhere. Without a doubt, the vast body of international research over the past 40+ years indicates that the best way to teach a child to recognise words is by systematic synthetic phonics or SSP. Research into phonics is a key part of what is commonly referred to as 'The Science of Reading' and, like other areas of research, it is continually being updated as the findings of new studies are published and, in turn, our understanding is redefined. The findings of research into phonics were historically included in landmark reports from the National Reading Panel 2000[2] in the US and the Rose Review of 2006[3] in the UK.

Models of Reading

How a child learns to read and develops into a fluent reader is described in a number of models. There is 'The Simple View of Reading' (Gough and Tunmer 2010)[4], 'The Five Pillars of Reading' (National Reading Panel 2000)[5], 'The Four-Part Processor' (Moats & Tolman 2019)[6], and Scarborough's 'Reading Rope' (2001)[7]. Although there are subtle differences between these models, the main tenets are the same and it is worth looking more closely at one of them. The Reading Rope is an excellent way to consider reading in its widest sense. Scarborough described becoming a reader as akin to the making of a rope – fibres (aspects of learning) are intertwined into bigger strands (key areas of learning) which in turn are intertwined to make a strong rope (a fluent reader) over time.

The two main strands or key areas of learning in Scarborough's Rope are:

- **Language Comprehension**, and

- **Word Recognition** (reading printed words).

These strands are in turn are made up of the following:

Language Comprehension

- Background Knowledge – subject-specific knowledge
- Vocabulary – breadth, linkage
- Language Structure – syntax and semantics
- Verbal Reasoning – drawing conclusions
- Literacy Knowledge – print concepts, genres

Word Recognition

- Phonological Awareness - syllables, phonemes, blending, segmenting, manipulation
- Decoding – applied knowledge of the alphabetic code
- Automaticity – reading words 'apparently instantly' or 'on sight'

The rope shows us that reading is not 'just phonics'. Comprehensive reading instruction should and does include *all* the fibres of both strands, although these are not necessarily all delivered in the same lesson. The teaching of language comprehension in schools is much less obvious than the teaching of phonics, as aspects are not usually taught in discrete lessons. Instead, they are taught across the curriculum and embedded within it.

For example, good language structure is modelled at 'story-time' when an adult reads an appropriate book aloud to the children and background knowledge is taught in subject area lessons through a broad and balanced overarching curriculum.

For the moment, though, let's focus on the word recognition strand and how we can teach this effectively.

The Alphabetic Code – Concepts and Knowledge

One of the key and consistent findings that has come out of the research is that the most effective way to teach reading is to take time to teach the word recognition strand, which is the foundation. The three fibres making up word recognition are taught together in a discrete session commonly referred to as a 'phonics lesson'.

In phonics lessons children learn to 'decode' the words on the page. The word decode is used because written language is considered to be a code – a code that uses the alphabet and speech sounds in the context of written words. In fact, the alphabetic code is bidirectional; it is reversible. We *decode* words to read them and *encode* words to spell them. Phonics lessons should include instruction in both reading and spelling and this book covers both of these activities.

So how does this alphabetic code work?

When we say a word we say lots of sounds in rapid succession, which we hear as a single spoken entity. In the alphabetic code, the sounds in the spoken word are isolated and identified and each one is represented on paper by a visual figure, which we call a letter. (Note that some sounds are represented by a small group of letters rather than a single one.) So, 'the code' is the relationship between the speech sounds (known more formally as **phonemes**) in spoken words and the letter or a small group of letters (known more formally as **graphemes**) in written words.

For example, when we say the word 'sat', we say three sounds or phonemes:

/s/ /a/ /t/

which we represent by the letters or graphemes

s a t

We could say that letters (or graphemes) represent sounds in written words. This is the first concept about the code that children need to understand. Work at this level is often referred to as 'basic' or 'initial' code. In the early stages of reading instruction children do lots of work at this simple one-to-one correspondence level (one phoneme – one letter) so that they are familiar with the idea of 'the code' and how it works.

*Note that there is a convention that phonemes are always written within forward slashes, e.g. /m/ as in **m**an, /sh/ as in **sh**op, /ai/ as in angel, /ee/ as in **ea**t etc.*

There are 42-44 phonemes in English words, the exact number depending on regional accent and pronunciation. It would be wonderful if the code had a simple one-to-one correspondence, as described above, for each sound. Imagine just 44 sounds and 44 bespoke graphemes to learn. That would be relatively easy and not too far away from the experience of learners of some other languages such as Finnish. Unfortunately, English doesn't work like this, and things get considerably more complicated.

Some sounds can be represented by graphemes made up of more than one letter.

For example, in the word 'pick' there are three sounds:

/p/ /i/ /k/

represented by the graphemes

p i **ck**

the /k/ sound being represented by the grapheme **ck**.

So, we have 3 sounds, 3 graphemes (as we'd expect) but 4 letters.

In fact, some sounds are represented by graphemes made up of 3 or even 4 letters, as in these words:

night   /n/ /ie/ /t/   n **igh** t

drought   /d/ /r/ /ou/ /t/   d r **ough** t

This is the second concept children need to understand about the code; some graphemes are made up of more than one letter. At this stage the code is often referred to as 'advanced' or 'extended' code.

To further complicate things for the beginner reader, there are more things in the mix. Some sounds are represented by not just one, but several different graphemes. For example, all the words below contain the sound /ee/ which is represented by the highlighted graphemes:

gr**ee**n   tr**ea**t   b**e**   bod**y**

These are the most common graphemes for /ee/ but there are others. This is the third concept children need to understand about the code; some sounds are represented by more than one grapheme. This is sometimes referred to as variation in the code.

But there's more. Some graphemes represent more than one sound. For example, all the words below contain the grapheme **ea**:

gr**ea**t   br**ea**d   m**ea**t

In these words, **ea** represents the sounds /ai/ /e/ and /ee/. This is the fourth concept children need to understand about the code and it is sometimes referred to as overlap in the code.

It's little wonder that beginner and developing readers find learning to read so difficult!

Of course, this is something of a simplification. Linguists, who study speech and language, would view things differently, pointing out that spoken words are in fact the coarticulation of sounds and that letters can also be grouped as units of meaning within words. However, as a working model used as the basis of constructing structured reading instruction for beginner and developing readers, it works extremely well. This simplified view of written language makes learning to read (and spell) accessible for young children starting out and for those with special educational needs and disabilities (SEND) / additional needs.

Skills

As well as learning about the alphabetic code and building their knowledge of it, children also need to learn some key skills so that they can *use* it, not just to read, but also to spell. These skills are:
- the phonological skill of identifying syllables in words and
- the phonemic skills of
    - isolating phonemes in spoken words,
    - blending phonemes to make a spoken word,
    - segmenting words into phonemes and
    - phoneme manipulation (sliding phonemes in and out of words).

Children need to be taught these skills and given lots of opportunities to practise and apply them in the context of letters and words. Teaching these skills is built into phonics programmes from the start and is a consistent feature of lessons until children have achieved mastery.

Moving Towards an Evidence-led Approach

The journey from research to teacher practice is not a straightforward one and it takes time for ideas to find their way into the classroom. The reading acquisition of children with complex needs has not been the subject of intense research activity until relatively recently, so we are playing catch up at this moment in time.

There are some historically held beliefs about learners with complex needs that have persisted in special schools but do not appear to hold up to scrutiny now that we have access to more evidence.

Historically, assumptions were made that phonics is too complex for SEND pupils to navigate, learn and use but actually it can be made accessible to pupils with a range of needs and where it is, they can find success.

It has also been assumed that children with complex needs need something different because they 'learn differently', often being described as 'visual learners'. The idea that there are lots of different ways to learn has been around for a while and was popularised in the 1980s. However, there is no evidence that people learn in different ways. What we do experience are personal preferences for information to be presented to us in certain ways. But this does not go on to translate into different pathways of learning within the brain. Daniel Willingham[8] reviewed the research and determined that, "scientific support for these theories is lacking" and goes on to say that, "educators' time and energy are better spent on other theories that might aid instruction."

It was also assumed that some children with complex needs are unable to hear and access phonemes. If it were true, then the implication is that they *have* to learn to read visually – they would have to learn to recognise the shape of individual whole words rather than learning phonics. My experience as a practitioner is that children with complex SEND often need to be *explicitly taught* to 'work with phonemes'. They may not find it easy, they may need some teaching strategies that are new to some teachers, and it may take some time, but they can be taught to access phonemes with the right instruction.

These two views, that children with SEND learn differently and are unable to access phonemes, has resulted in many children never being given the opportunity to learn phonics and instead being taught to read whole words as 'sight words'. Let's explore this way of learning to read.

Read this word aloud...

sound

Beguiling, isn't it? You just looked at it, knew it and apparently instantaneously said it with no 'sounding out'. Competent adult readers like you and I read like this, and this is what we want for our pupils. Intuitively we feel that we just 'look' and 'say'.

Now try reading this word...

graphophonemic

Not quite the same experience. You were probably able to read it relatively quickly but needed to think more consciously about it. Did you notice yourself scanning the graphemes and thinking about phonemes and syllables? Did you blend sounds and syllables? In other words, did you use phonics? When we encounter words, we have not seen before, especially long words, we need to decode on a more conscious level.

So, what is going on in the brain when we learn to read?

The pathway involved within the brain is increasingly well known thanks to research. It is one that enables us, as competent adult readers, to read the 20-60,000 words that we know, apparently instantaneously. It also allows us to read words we have never seen before, also relatively quickly, like graphophonemic *(graphophonemic awareness is 'the ability to match phonemes and graphemes')*.

The initial pathway of reading in the brain is a phonological one. Later, connections are made between orthography (spelling patterns) and semantics (the meaning of the word). Making explicit connections between phonemes and graphemes during our phonics teaching supports learning to read via this pathway.

It *is* possible to learn to recognise words visually and singly as whole words or word shapes – sometimes referred to as learning 'sight words'. So, let's compare the two possible routes.

If we learn words via the visual route they are stored as images in long term visual memory. Storage capacity is limited so the number of words a child can recognise is limited and may be severely limited for children with complex needs.

Words learnt via phonics are stored in long term phonological memory. Storage capacity for words via this phonological route is, as far as we know, huge so there is potentially no limit to the number of words that can be learnt. This already sounds like the better option

In addition to this, the visual pathway does not provide the child with the flexibility of using what they already know about words to read new, unknown words when they meet them. This is because the phonological route includes a process called orthographic mapping. Orthographic mapping is the overlaying of graphemes onto corresponding phonemes (Ehri)[9] and it enables the brain to taking reading that stage further, to notice and access phoneme strings which can be used to work out unknown words (Share)[10].

So, the phonological route, i.e. learning phonics, enables children to potentially read thousands of words and use their knowledge to read unknown words. The visual route, i.e. the whole word or sight word approach, enables pupils to learn a limited number of words and does not assist them to read unknown words. Without a doubt phonics is the better option.

Teaching phonics within a simple conceptual framework via a structured teaching sequence of sounds that incorporates teaching all the skills, concepts and knowledge the child needs, is the best way to teach children to read and spell.

The Wider View of Reading

We know that it is important that time is dedicated to teaching pupils to recognise words and phonics is the best way to do this. This is the very foundation of reading. After all, if we cannot decode or 'lift the words' from the page in the first place, we cannot ever hope to understand what is written. But let's pull back the focus and once again think of Scarborough's Reading Rope in its entirety.

Learners with complex needs are very likely to have difficulties with one or more of the aspects of the language comprehension strand and this will impact on reading. In special schools, teachers are familiar with these aspects (although not their place in reading development) and are comfortable with making them a focus of the curriculum, planning targeted activities, and delivering interventions guided by professional colleagues such as speech and language therapists.

It would make sense that this work could be tied in some way to reading instruction and a good way to do this is when you are listening to a child read. A common feature of phonics instruction is to read a decodable (phonically controlled) book matched to the child's level of phonic knowledge and skill. There is an opportunity here to pull in activities that work on the language comprehension aspects as they naturally arise.

This might include:

- vocabulary, with a focus on any words that are unknown to the child and a mind to expand the bank of words they have heard and know the meaning of,
- language structure, with a focus on simple sentence structure, moving on to more complex aspects of spoken language,
- background knowledge, with a focus on plugging any gaps in their knowledge and experience of the subject matter,
- verbal reasoning, with a focus on reading and re-reading texts and talking 'about and around the subject' to read between the lines and draw conclusions about the text.

We should always be mindful of this bigger picture of reading instruction when teaching. This could be described as 'Teaching The Rope'.

Phonics Programmes

Now that we are familiar with Scarborough's Reading Rope, we can see that perhaps the term 'phonics' programme is a misnomer, covering as it does phonemic and phonological awareness, phonics and developing automaticity. Perhaps 'word recognition' programme might be more accurate. So, let's take some time to consider the programmes that are on offer.

There are a range of commercially produced phonics programmes that have been developed so that teachers do not have to spend a lot of time creating their own. These programmes have features in common, including starting with the simplest elements and building up to more complex elements, an incremental and cumulative progression or teaching sequence and a scope that covers all the concepts, skills and knowledge needed to manage the code to read and spell.

That said, not everything that is described as phonics is the same and it is worth looking into the different types you might come across, especially if you are choosing a programme to use with your pupils with complex needs.

Types of Phonics Instruction

There are several different types of phonics instruction.

Analytic phonics is often described as a 'top-down' approach. Pupils start with the whole word and then break it down into its constituent parts, analysing it, to find out about the relationship between the phonemes and graphemes in the word. Critics of this type of phonics state that the choice of which words are analysed is often dependent on the text the child is given. This means that the words studied do not form a structured, cumulative sequence that enables pupils to work through all the code starting with the simplest elements first. Analogy phonics is similar but focuses on patterns of graphemes that appear in words e.g. onset and rime and word families - the beginnings and endings of words such as mate, gate, rate etc.

Synthetic phonics is often described as a 'bottom-up' strategy. Pupils start with the smallest units of words, phonemes and graphemes, and learn about the relationship between the two. They use these to build or synthesise words. It is relatively easy to create a structured, cumulative sequence, starting with the simplest elements and building up to more complex ones. Programmes that do this are called systematic, synthetic phonics programmes or SSP and it is this type of phonics that research suggests is the most effective for children learning to read and spell.

Linguistic phonics is systematic with a good scope and sequence and is also synthetic since it considers how sounds and graphemes are built into words. The difference between conventional SSP (which, confusingly, is generally simply referred to as 'synthetic phonics') and linguistic phonics, is rooted in the direction in which the code is presented during instruction. In synthetic phonics the code is taught with the emphasis on the grapheme and how it is represented by a phoneme. In linguistic phonics the code is taught with the emphasis on the phoneme and how it is represented by a grapheme. Linguistic phonics is sometimes also referred to as 'speech to print'. This is not a particularly helpful description as it gives the impression that all the activities in a programme are phoneme to grapheme. Of course, both synthetic and linguistic phonics teach in both directions. We decode to read - 'print to speech' and encode to spell - 'speech to print'. During instruction, teachers of linguistic phonics use language that subtly references the direction in which written language was created, i.e. from spoken language. Those who initially created the code were driven by the need to convert their spoken message / story / plans / philosophy into a visual system that others who knew the code could decrypt and understand. So, linguistic phonics reinforces the nature and logic of the English language.

One of the benefits to SEND pupils of linguistic phonics is the logic of the teaching sequence. Conventional synthetic phonics programmes that focus on the grapheme first and then the phoneme, structure their teaching sequence based on the frequency with which the grapheme appears in words. Although, this makes sense on an intuitive level, it comes with some problems. This results in the graphemes being taught in a somewhat scattered sequence. A child may learn that ai represents the phoneme /ai/ one week but will have to wait several weeks to learn that ay also represents the phoneme /ai/. In the intervening weeks pupils learn about other graphemes and their sounds and this may be confusing to pupils with SEND.

On the other hand, linguistic phonics focuses on the phoneme and the child learns all the graphemes that can represent it at the same time. This presents the child with a schema (mental plan) of the relationship between the phoneme and its graphemes. The child does not have to make the connections themself by linking learning that happened several weeks or months previously. Linguistic phonics sets up pupils to easily create a cognitive map of the alphabetic code as they learn about more phonemes over time. Mainstream learners may be able to make these connections themselves but for our learners with SEND, this represents a significant cognitive demand. Linguistic phonics is a more accessible way into the code for learners with SEND.

Choosing a programme

Not all programmes are designed and written for learners with moderate to severe and complex needs. In fact, the majority are aimed at mainstream learners in the first few years of school, and this presents a number of issues for teachers of children with more than mild needs.

When selecting a programme for learners with complex needs, look out for the following features in terms of presentation:

- resources are clear and linear in format (working left to right and down the page), so it is easy for pupils to know where to start and how to work through them,
- a single task is presented on a worksheet rather than lots of different tasks,
- resources are clutter free with no distracting, unnecessary illustrations (not related to the task), use of unusual fonts or writing at jaunty angles,
- resources, including illustrations and language, are age appropriate for the learners or age neutral.

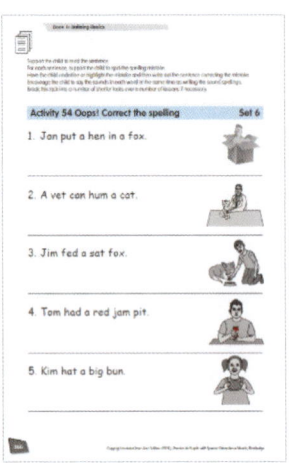 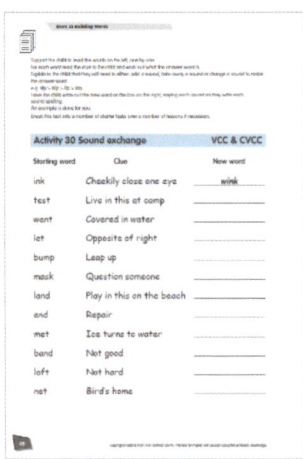 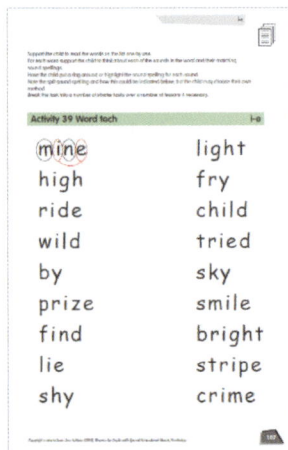

Also look out for the following features in terms of the breadth of available activities and accessibility:

- at each stage in the programme there is a broad range of activities to give plenty of opportunities for learning, practise and application of the phonics they are learning, as repetition is important for these learners,
- pupils can move through the programme at a pace appropriate to their needs via small incremental steps of learning,
- activities are adapted or suggestions given for adaptations to meet the needs of a range of learners,
- access strategies are easy to incorporate into activities and resources.

Incidental Phonics

As well as teaching phonics via a structured programme, it is important to make the most of any opportunity to embed what the child is learning in their phonics lessons across the curriculum. Whenever a child asks for support to read a word or spell a word, it presents us with a chance to reinforce what they already know about phonics and even teach them a little more.

This kind of 'in the moment' instruction is often called incidental phonics and is important as it demonstrates to the child the relevance and use of phonics in a range of situations, not just in phonics lessons.

For example, a child asks for help to spell the word 'weight' in a science lesson. The teacher knows he has worked on the sounds /w/ and /t/ but not the sound /ai/. The child is encouraged to say the first sound /w/ and write down the grapheme that matches w. Then the child moves on and identifies (with support if required) the next sound in the word /ai/. The teacher then gently interrupts and says, "You haven't done this yet but one of the ways we can write it is like this." The teacher then writes the grapheme eigh on a whiteboard or piece of paper and the child copies it, saying the sound /ai/ as they write. The child then says the next sound in the word and matches the grapheme t to it. In this way they write the word weight.

Let's look at another example, this time from a social situation. A child asks for help to read the word 'bread' during a visit to a café with her class. The teacher knows she has worked on the sounds /b/ /r/ and /d / so should recognize the b r and d graphemes, but does not know that the sound /e/ can be represented by the grapheme ea. The child is encouraged to look at each grapheme, say the matching sound and blend through the word. She can blend /b/ and /r/ and then is gently interrupted and is told that ea is a grapheme that represents /e/. After beginning again, she can use this new information and blend through to the end of the word /b//r//e/ /d/ "bread".

So, we have explored written language, the alphabetic code, phonics and how to teach reading and spelling but at this point, we have to acknowledge an uncomfortable truth. Written language and how it works is fixed. The alphabetic code is the same for all of us. We are required to make adjustments and adaptations for our learners with SEND but we cannot change the code itself on their behalf, however complex their needs and however much we'd like to. They have to learn the code and how it works to be able to manage and use it, just like their peers. Our duty is to make adjustments to how we teach it so that pupils can access it and learn about the code.

The question we need to focus on then is not '**what** do we teach our pupils with SEND?' but '**how** do we make it accessible to pupils with a range of SEND and instructional needs?'

> **Summary**
> - Reading is a combination of language comprehension and word recognition.
> - Written language is viewed as an alphabetic code with a relationship between the sounds in spoken words and the letters on the page.
> - In phonics lessons children learn concepts, skills and knowledge that enables them to manage the alphabetic code for reading and spelling.
> - Research indicates that children are best taught to read and spell via systematic, synthetic phonics.
> - Learning to read whole words visually (sight words) is not an effective way to learn to read.

3. Pupils with Complex Profiles

This book focuses on the delivery of phonics to pupils of all ages with a range of educational needs and disabilities, specifically:

- pupils with a physical disability or disabilities,
- pupils who are pre- or nonverbal / non-speaking,
- pupils who are both pre- or nonverbal / non-speaking *and* have a physical disability or disabilities,
- pupils with sensory needs - visual impairment, hearing impairment and multisensory impairment,
- pupils with sensory processing needs,
- pupils with processing difficulties.

You will notice that this list is a description of barriers to access to the curriculum and is not a list of conditions or diagnostic labels. None of the above need be a barrier to a child learning to read, spell and express themselves in a written form. What is important is to consider how their disability impacts on them. With this knowledge, adjustments and adaptations can be made to enable access to learning and decisions can be made about what strategies will be beneficial. This is the key – adjustments and adaptations to enable access to the curriculum.

A child's cognition and learning needs have a bearing on their potential for becoming a successful reader and writer. It is useful to look at their individual profile of cognitive strengths and weaknesses. To be ready to learn to read and spell, children need to be able to:

- recognise, differentiate, process, remember and recall auditory information, specifically speech sounds or phonemes,
- understand that visual figures or symbols can 'stand for' or represent something,
- recognize, differentiate, process, remember and recall visual information, specifically letter forms.

Children also need to understand or be able to be taught to understand:

- that spoken words convey meaning,
- that spoken words are made up of sounds (phonemes),
- that the sounds (phonemes) in words always occur in a consistent sequence to convey the required meaning,
- that a sequence of words conveys a greater meaning.

Learning to read and spell also involves introducing some new key concepts about the alphabetic code and how it works. The child should be able to learn, understand and work with these, implicitly, as part of their developing reading and spelling skills.

Children need to be able to learn and understand that:

- letters are symbols that represent sounds (phonemes),

- some sounds are represented by a group of letters rather than just one letter,
- some sounds are represented by more than one grapheme and
- some graphemes represent more than one sound.

The takeaway message here is the importance of knowing and understanding an individual child's profile of cognitive strengths and weaknesses to decide whether they are realistically able to begin to learn to read and spell and how to plan for their access. The majority of children with complex needs will be able to start instruction on an appropriate structured phonics programme.

For a very small number of children with profound and multiple learning difficulties (PMLD) teaching reading may not be appropriate if they are working at an early developmental stage. The Reading Framework (DfE 2021)[1] states, "A very few children with profound and multiple learning difficulties (PMLD) might not be able to access direct literacy instruction but might access alternative activities to teach children how letters correspond to sounds within the context of a pre-formal sensory curriculum."

This does not mean that these children should not exposed to text and books. They need access to a rich literacy environment just like their peers. Schools should be aspirational for these children and consider ways to 'prime' them for phonics instruction that they may be able to access at a later point. Providing phonemic awareness activities that incorporate letters and words also enables teachers to identify and fast track those children who are cognitively able and ready to learn to read but whose physical and communication disabilities mask this.

The Resources in this Book

There is a range of commercially available specialist software that can be used to enhance phonics instruction but describing these is not the scope of this book. The purpose of this book is to show teachers how to use low-tech solutions to accessibility. These are easy to make, easy to use, are portable and are cost effective.

Pupils will need time to become familiar with the strategies described in this book; familiar with the resources and how to use them. Before diving straight into using them in phonics activities, use them for 'soft' activities with fun, easy tasks that allow children to understand how the strategies work and practise using them until they are comfortable with them.

Similarly, teachers themselves will need to practise using the strategies so delivery is smooth. Practising with a colleague will enable teachers to develop familiarity with a working protocol and develop their own 'patter' to go alongside the strategy so that activities are consistently presented to pupils for their benefit.

It should also be noted that teachers will also need time to prepare the additional resources required for these pupils before each lesson.

Lesson Planning

When planning a phonics lesson or session for pupils with complex needs, it is important to bear in mind that:

- lessons can be intense because of the frequency and length of pupil-teacher interactions, even when working in a group – be aware that pupils may tire so consider beginning with short sessions, gradually extending learning time, and planning in a low intensity activity mid-way which gives a pupil an opportunity to rest,
- activities will take longer to deliver and complete because of the nature of the strategies and the procedures involved,
- overall, it will take longer for complex pupils to work through any programme because of the additional delivery time involved in using access strategies.

Summary
- Children with complex learning profiles may have several barriers to accessing phonics.
- It is important to know and understand a child's individual profile of needs.
- The key is enabling access to phonics by using a range of strategies as described in this book.

4. Access for Pupils with a Physical Disability

The impact of a physical disability or disabilities may be on a child's gross and/or fine motor skills, both of which are likely to impact on access to the curriculum.

Seating and Positioning

It may come as a surprise that gross motor skills are important for learning to read, or learning anything in a classroom situation. Both the lower and upper body are involved in the maintenance of a comfortable upright sitting position for working. If a child is unable to easily maintain good posture and positioning, they may experience discomfort or pain and are likely to be distracted from learning tasks, frequently shifting in their seat to find ease and comfort.

All children should be seated on appropriately sized desks and chairs such that their bodies are able to maintain the optimal positioning, with the body making 90° angles at the base of the spine / hips and at the knees. Both feet should be flat on the floor (or on a footrest) providing a stable base, with the child sitting with their back well supported by the chair back. Check that pupils are able to sit comfortably and provide furniture that puts them in a good seating position. Be prepared to be creative – have a range of seating options in the classroom or use table risers and footrests to achieve this. Encourage changes of position from time to time so pupils can realign their posture.

It is common for younger children to be asked to sit on the floor for 'carpet time'. Be aware that children with physical disabilities may find it difficult to independently lower themselves to the floor, sit comfortably for any length of time and raise themselves to standing, so sitting on the carpet can be a challenge in itself. If they are expected to spend a long time on the floor doing work on whiteboards, for example, there may be an impact on attention and learning. These children may do better seated on a chair (with some friends doing likewise, so that they do not feel singled out).

Children with significant physical disabilities may need support to manage posture, in the form of specialist seating systems. Occupational therapists are involved in the assessment of seating and positioning and subsequent recommendations for specialist chairs.

Writing

If movement and control of the shoulders, arms, hands, wrist and fingers is impaired then a child is likely to find it difficult to hold and manipulate objects with much precision, or indeed at all. When writing, children need to hold a pen firmly with a stable pen grip and make accurate, controlled movements to form the letters on the page.

When beginning to learn their 'sounds and letters' at the start of instruction, children also learn how to form and write the letter shapes. Research indicates that there is a link between physically hand-writing the letter forms and learning the associated sounds Wiley and Rapp[11].

Wherever possible, children should be given the opportunity to learn and practise letter formation alongside phonics instruction.

Some children benefit from using adapted writing implements to enable or support a functional, stable grip and there is a wide range available. These include:

- pens and pencils with a wider diameter so they are easier to grip,
- pens and pencils with a triangular body to gently encourage a tripod grip,
- pencil grips that attach on to pencils and support optimal positioning of the fingers in a tripod grip,
- ridged or spiky pencil grips that provide greater sensory feedback, so a child has greater awareness of the position of the pencil in relation to the paper when forming the letter shape, and
- pencils made of soft graphite so a child who cannot apply much pressure when writing can make a mark.

For some children, their fine motor skills are such that they are unable to hold and manipulate a pen and writing is not likely to be a long-term strategy for recording work. It is important to give these children at least some experience of forming individual letters, if possible. Using any drawing or painting app on a tablet will enable the pupil to form letters and see the result of their movements. Pupils should be encouraged to say the matching sound at the same time as writing the grapheme.

Recording Work

Now let's think about how a child might record their work independently if they are unable to handwrite. Typing may be an appropriate long-term strategy. There is a huge range of external keyboards that can be used with a laptop. Some have super large keys to make the individual letters visible and provide a bigger target to aim at and press. Some have a key guard (a metal grid over the top of the keyboard with holes that match the keys) that help if the child has difficulty targeting their finger to press a specific key or has a tremor.

Additional equipment such as arm and wrist rests and laptop slopes may be helpful and there is a wide range of alternative mice available to suit individual needs e.g. simplified mouse (single button / no scroll wheel), tracker ball and joystick.

There is also a range of 3rd party on-screen keyboards available for tablets and touchscreens. In most, the layout, colour, font, size and other features can be adjusted in the settings as can access to predictive text, which can (usefully) be turned off. If the child is able to type, then typing could be used as the recording strategy in any situation, including phonics lessons. The keyboard should be set so that it does not give any auditory feedback i.e. does not say the letter names or the basic sounds when the child types a letter. The child should be encouraged to say each sound at the same time as pressing the key to type the grapheme. When working at an advanced level, where graphemes are represented by a number of letters, the child should say the sound on typing the first letter and say nothing on typing the remaining letters of the grapheme.

For those children who can isolate fingers, then learning to touch type is recommended as this will speed up typing in the long term. However, some children may only be able to target and type one finger at a time. Indeed, some children may not be able to do this. These children may be able to use a continuous gliding motion with one finger moving from letter to letter within a word using an appropriate keyboard such as Swiftkey.

For other children the use of speech to text software may be beneficial for extended pieces of writing.

Desktop Activities

Pupils with fine motor difficulties benefit from access to adapted activities in phonics lessons, in the form of desktop manipulatives. These are often card-based resources that the child can move around the tabletop with relatively little force or movement required – they may only need to push, pull or sometimes turn cards over. Their usefulness is a proportional to the ease with which pupils are able to move them around in response to a task.

Examples of desktop manipulatives are:

- **Games**

Both board and card games can be a great way of getting pupils to read and spell (mostly single) words. They are engaging and fun but also provide an opportunity for repetition and overlearning, which is important for learners with SEND. Games can be incorporated into lessons at any stage of a phonics programme.

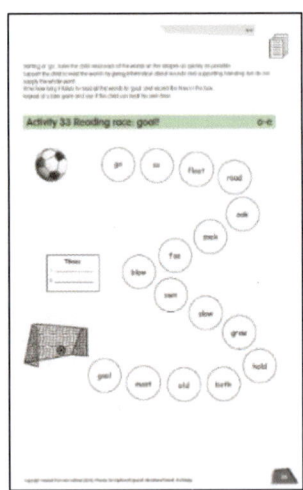
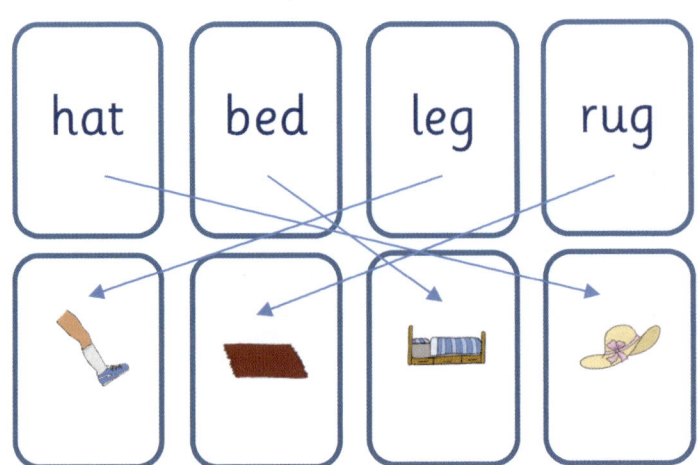

- **Letter Sliders**

Letter sliders are a simple desktop manipulative that enables a pupil to build (spell) a word and then change the word by swapping a phoneme and sliding in the correct grapheme. These are great for practising phoneme manipulation and can be used at any stage in a phonics programme.

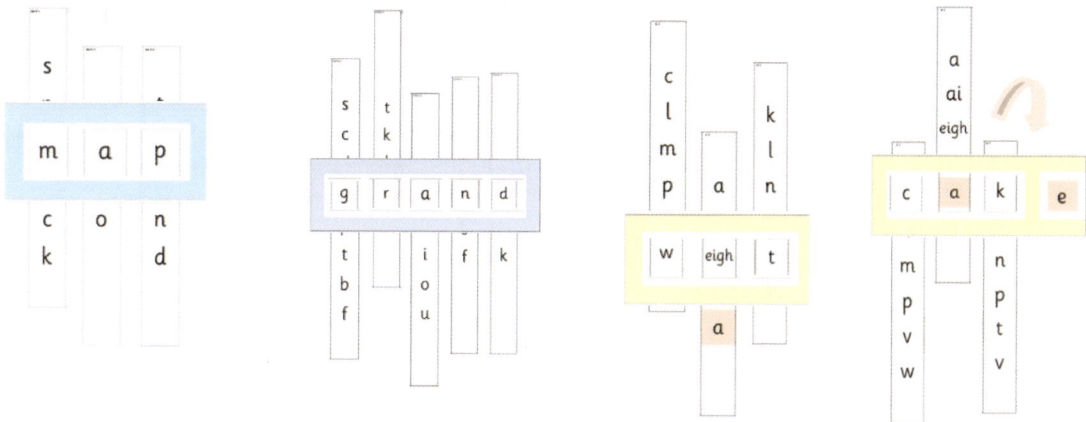

- **Movable Alphabets**

The movable alphabet is an extremely useful manipulative. There are a range of options available including, wooden, plastic or foam letters, textured letters and letters printed on card. These can be used for activities that involve both reading and spelling words, but it is particularly useful for spelling.

By offering the pupil a choice of letters, they can segment the word and match a letter for each sound. Draw lines on a white board or piece of paper, support the child to segment the word and move the matching grapheme card for each sound to build the word. In the example below the child has been asked to spell the word 'pen'. You can see how they build up the word sound by sound.

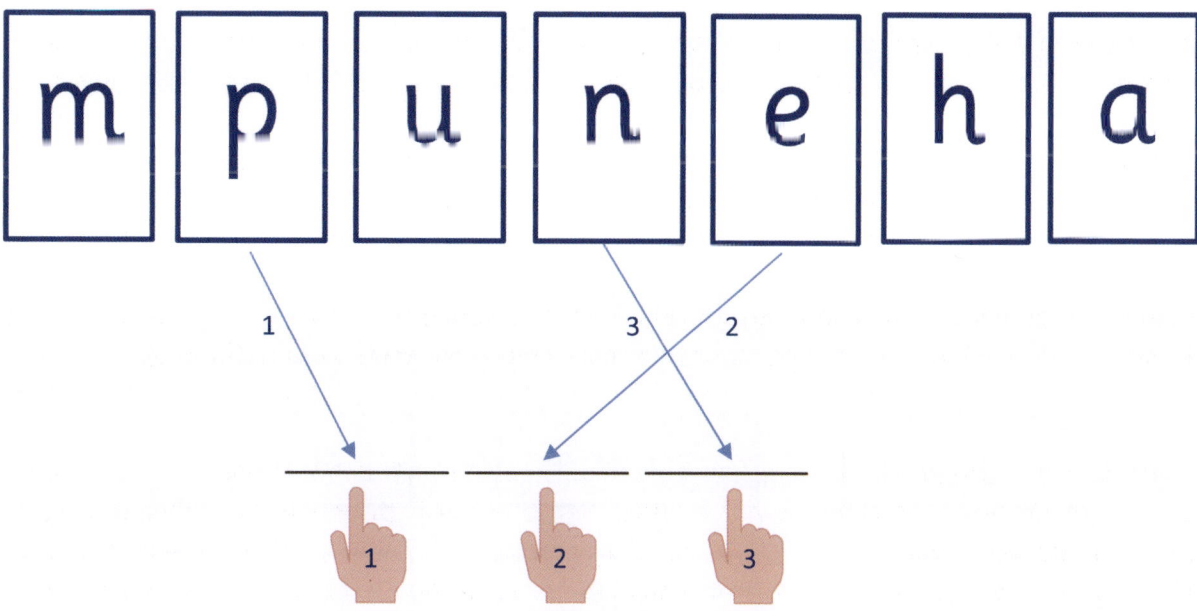

Commercially produced resources tend to focus on single letters rather than graphemes containing more than one letter. This is fine at the beginning of instruction but not as children move through a programme. Card based movable alphabets come into their own here as they can be made to represent the full range of graphemes in the alphabetic code. In the next example, the child is required to spell the word 'spell'.

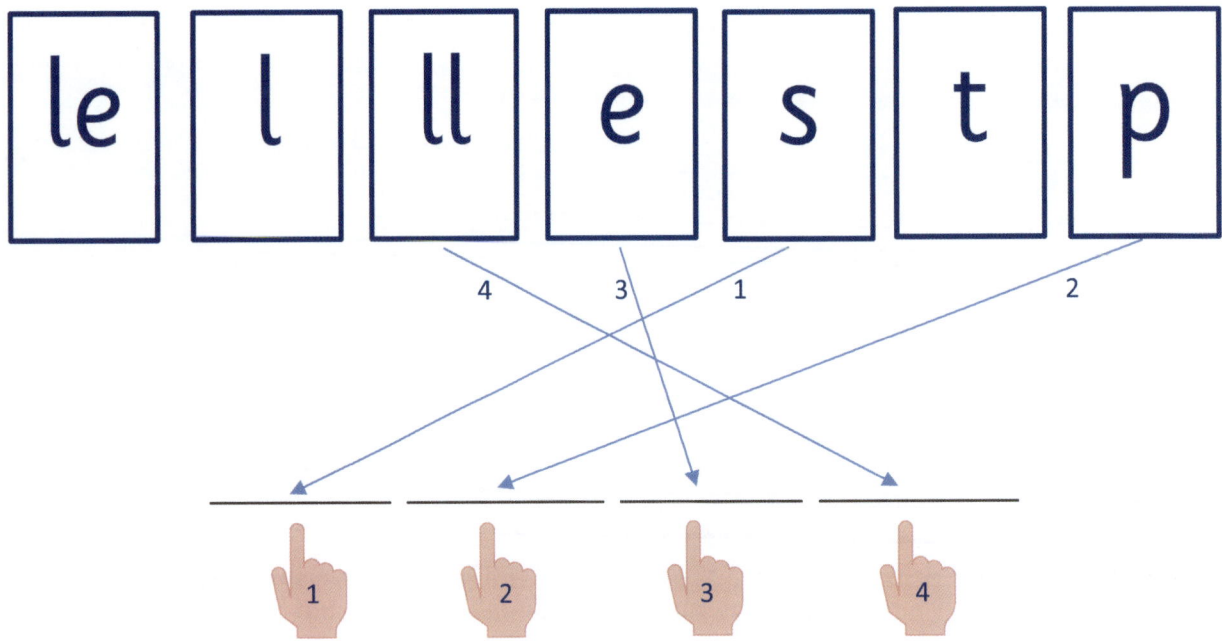

A movable alphabet is included in the resources section in the Appendix the end of this book. The tiles have a blank space in the lower part of the tile so the child can move the card and still see the grapheme.

- **Word Cards**

Word cards are versatile as they can be used for reading words as an activity in itself or as a part of a sorting activity, which often features in phonics instruction:

- reading activity – place a number of different words on the desk and ask the pupil to read and find a specific word, read the words as quickly as they can (then try to beat their own time), read and identify any words they don't know the meaning of (with a view to doing some vocabulary work) etc.

  For example, when working on the sound /ou/, ask the pupil to find the word 'town'.

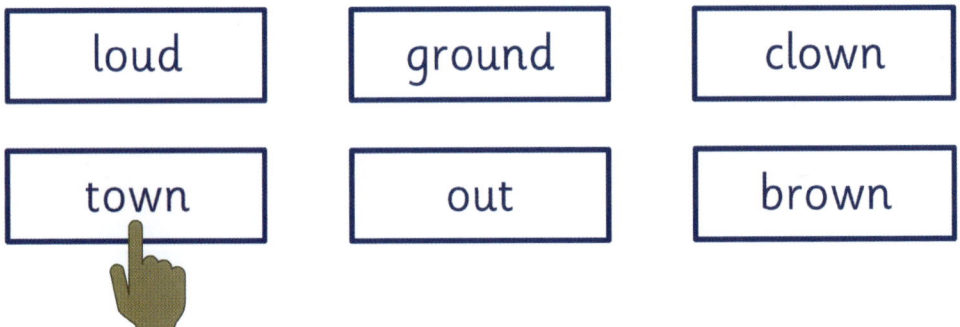

- sorting activity 1 – offer the child a set of word cards (all containing the same focus sound) shuffled randomly and ask them to sort the words into groups according to the *grapheme* representing the sound – this activity explores the variation in the alphabetic code,

22

e.g. investigating the sound /ch/

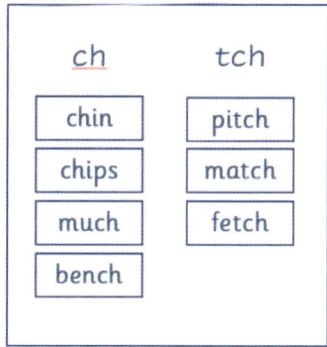

- sorting activity 2 – offer the child a set of word cards (all containing the same target grapheme) shuffled randomly and ask them to sort the words into groups according to the *sound* represented by the grapheme – this activity explores the overlap in the alphabetic code,

e.g. investigating the grapheme *ea*

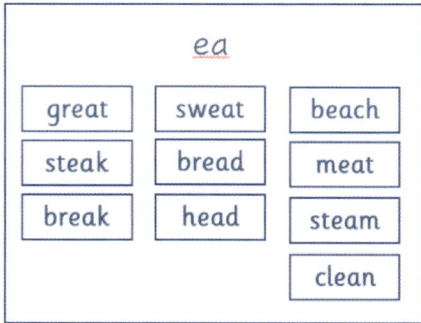

- **Word Cards for Sentence Building**

Word cards can also be used to build sentences matched to the phonics the child is working on in class.

For those that need support with word order (syntax) in sentences, the cards can be associated with a prompt question that in turn relates to the type of words they are (parts of speech). The addition of colour coding further highlights the relationship between the word, it's specific place in a sentence, syntax and meaning.

Here we see a sentence that is of a simple subject-verb-object-location format using the Rainbow Speakers[12] resources.

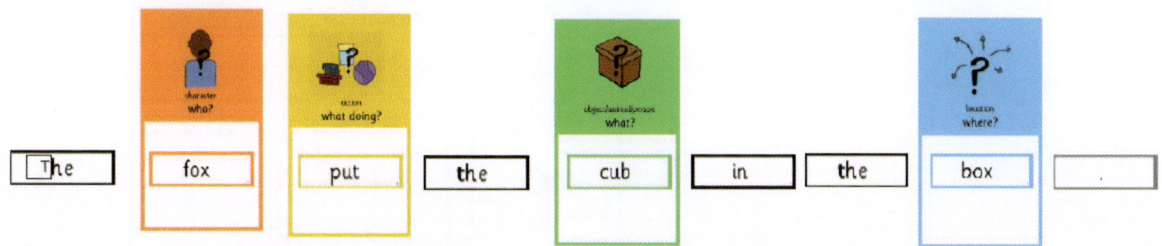

Worksheets

Worksheets are a common feature of phonics programmes, requiring pupils to write a response on paper.

Where single word answers are required, a child may spell the word using a moveable alphabet with the teacher acting as a scribe and writing their answer on the sheet, as in this example.

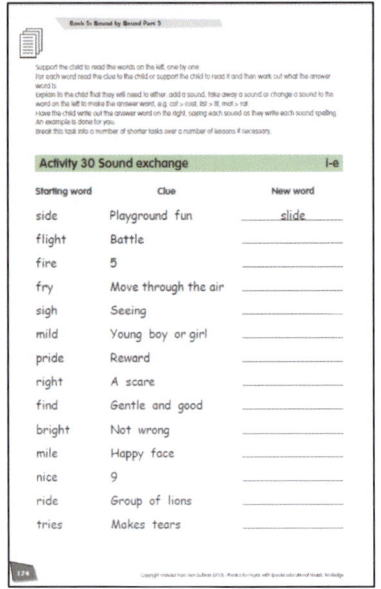

For a higher tech solution to worksheet access, there are apps, such as SnapType Pro, that enable the user to take a photograph and annotate the picture on screen. Simply photograph the worksheet and open it in the app. When the child touches the screen, a textbox opens up and the child can type in their answer in the appropriate space on the page. This can be saved and printed out so there is a permanent record.

For some pupils presenting them with a worksheet full of task items can be overwhelming and a source of anxiety. Linear format worksheets can be easily adapted as they can be cut into single item strips or worksheet 'snippets' and presented in this way item by item.

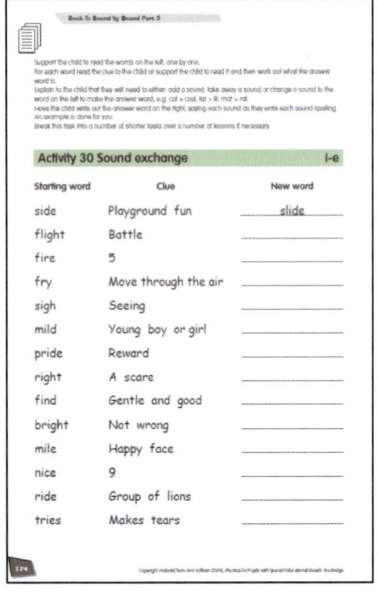
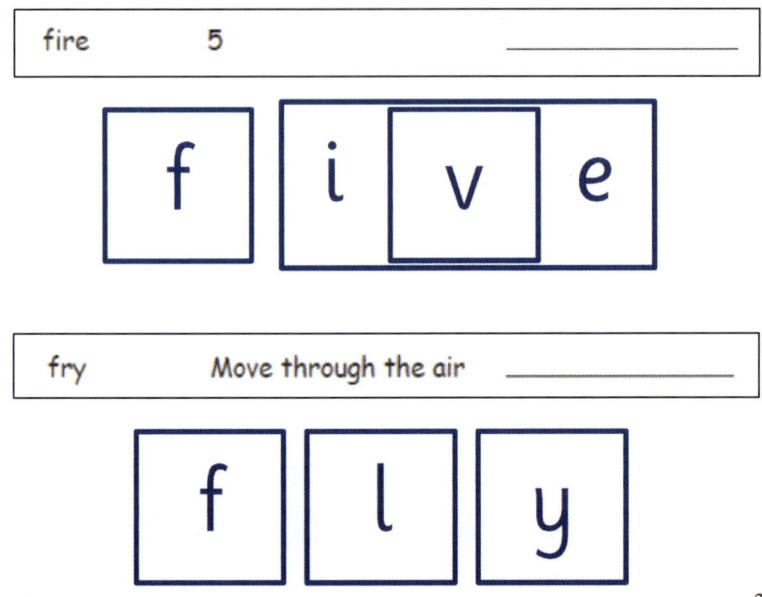

24

Over time, with careful planning, pupils can work through more and more of the worksheet in small accessible snippets.

When working in this way, it is important to make sure that coverage of different aspects of phonics is even across a given timescale.

> **Summary**
> - Appropriate seating and positioning are important for children with a physical disability.
> - Handwriting may not be a child's long-term strategy for recording work.
> - Desktop manipulatives are useful when working with children with a physical disability and there is a range available.

5. Access for Pupils who are Preverbal or Nonverbal

This chapter focuses on meeting the needs of pupils who are pre- or non-verbal / non-speaking, those who, at this point in time, are unable to speak, choose not to speak or whose speech is difficult to understand. For these children the spoken word is not their usual method of communication, and they may be users of Augmentative and Alternative Communication (AAC), such as a symbol-based communication chart, communication book or voice output device, commonly called a talker.

There are many communication systems and devices available and incorporating them into phonics teaching poses a few problems. Inevitably, the number and range of words on a communication board, communication book or programmed into a pupil's device is limited and determined by functional communication needs rather than the needs of a phonics teaching sequence. This limits their potential use in phonics lessons. Additionally, the symbols have the word written underneath and if a child is asked to read a word and find the matching symbol there is the possibility that they could be matching words visually rather than actually reading. A further problem is apparent if using a voice output device for spelling. When the letter keys are pressed the talker often says the letter name, not the sound. Even if this is switched to saying the sounds, there are further complications when the child is working at the stage in instruction when they encounter graphemes made up of more than one letter. For example, if the child types the word play the ay grapheme will be spoken as two sounds /a/ /y/ rather than the single sound /ai/.

In response to this, this book focuses on low-tech strategies that can be uses to enable access to phonics activities. Generally speaking, during lessons pupils do not use their communication board, communication book or voice output device as part of instruction. That does not mean that pupils do not have access to their usual communication method. If pupils need to tell the teacher something unrelated to instruction, for example the need to use the bathroom, then they would, of course, use their board, book or device.

Thinking Voice

Although these pupils do not vocalise, it is important for them to understand that they do have 'a voice'. That voice is 'in their head' and can be rich and detailed. This is their 'thinking voice'. It is important to reference this throughout instruction as they will need to access this in a range of phonics activities.

To reinforce this, it is useful to use a visual prompt like this 'thinking voice' symbol:

A range of thinking voice symbols are included in the resources section in the Appendix at the end of this book.

When teaching the key skills of blending, segmenting and manipulating phonemes, the teacher models these processes for the child but soon encourages them to replicate these 'in their head' using their thinking voice. Of course, we cannot directly check that this is actually happening, but we can assess the outcome of an activity e.g. reading or spelling the word.

The Strategies

There are two key aspects to working with pupils who are pre- or nonverbal. Firstly, we need to use strategies that enable us to find out what the child knows about what we have been teaching them and secondly, we need to use strategies that enable them to tell us about their learning.

Finding out about a Child's Learning

To find out about the child's learning (what they know or can do) and to get answers to questions asked during instruction, we can use the following strategies which we will explore in more detail:

   a. offering a choice of auditory responses anchored to dots on a visual place marker (VPM)
   b. matching pictures to single words or phrases
   c. binary responses presented as symbols e.g. yes / no   good / not good
   d. number responses presented as symbols
   e. desktop manipulatives
   f. response to the teacher making a deliberate mistake – Big Oops!
   g. use of single message recording devices

a. Visual Place Markers

The use of a Visual Place Marker (VPM) is a very versatile strategy that enables pupils to communicate about their learning during phonics lessons.

A VPM is simply a series of coloured dots on a card. The teacher can assign a verbal 'item' to each dot and so offer a choice of possible answers to questions posed. The child recalls the auditory information and responds by pointing to the dot that matches their choice of answer. A two dot VPM is used to allow the child to become accustomed to the strategy before moving on to a three dot VPM to offer a greater level of challenge. some children may remain at the two dot level.

Let's look at how this works in practice. Imagine you ask a child to read the word 'man', but they are hesitant, and you need to step in to support. You need to find out if they know that the first letter represents the sound /m/. You point to the letter and ask, "What sound is this a picture of?"

Then **without saying anything else** (as this would be distracting) simply point to the blue dot and anchor a sound to it. *You are going to anchor a sound to each dot so think carefully about the choices you offer*. For this first dot the sound is /t/.

/t/

Then point to the red dot and anchor a sound to it /m/ and finally point to the yellow dot and anchor a sound to it /f/.

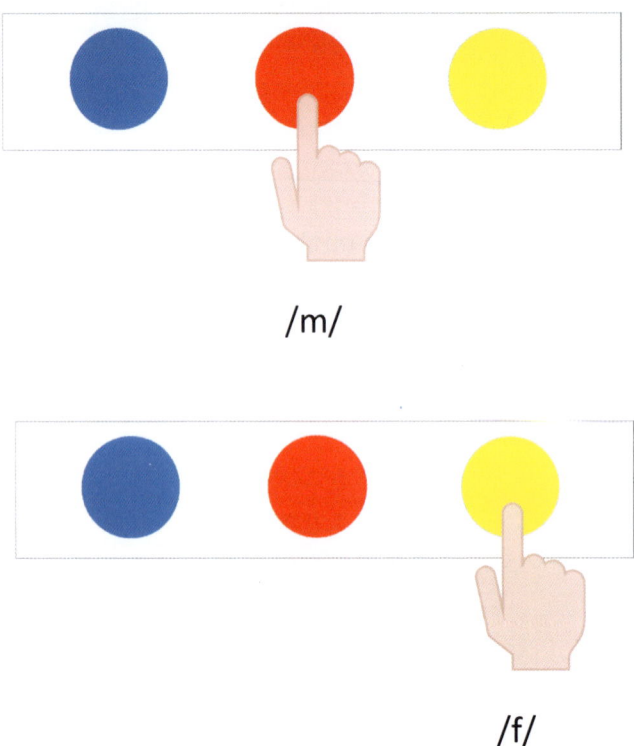

/m/

/f/

You can repeat these if you think necessary. The child then makes their choice and points to the dot that matches their answer.

In this case the child correctly points to the red dot and chooses the sound /m/. You know the child knows the first sound and can continue from there, working through the word encouraging the child to think about the sounds and blending them to get the word.

As well as anchoring sounds, you can also anchor spoken words. Here, you are asking the child to read this word.

You offer them some word choices anchored to the dots.

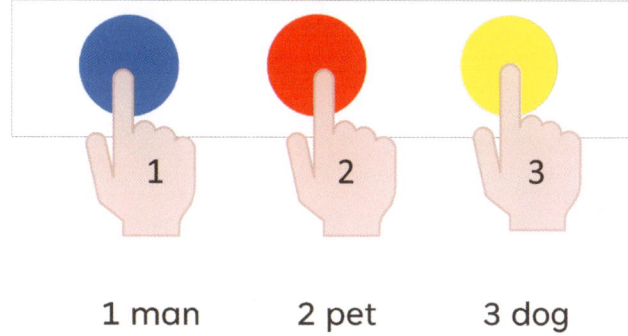

The child points to the yellow dot to identify the correct choice.

Actually, you can anchor *any* auditory information this way: sounds, words, phrases or sentences depending on the activity. This makes a VPM a very flexible strategy for working on reading. It can be used when carrying out focused work on specific phonemes and when reading single words, phrases and sentences. It can also be used when reading extended text on worksheets and in decodable readers.

A VPM can also be used when working on spelling. Let's take an example of a child working at the advanced code level.

The child is working on the phoneme /ai/ and is asked to spell the word rain. The word rain has three phonemes so start by drawing three lines on a whiteboard or piece of paper. This acts as a visual prompt (that three graphemes are required to spell the word), so we are looking to identify three sounds. You then take the child through the word, working step by step.

_____ _____ _____

Pointing to the first line ask the child, "What sound can you hear here in the word rain?" Say the word 'rain' as if modelling blending. As you say the word rain run your finger under all three lines taking care that as you say the word the position of your finger corresponds to the sound you are saying within the word.

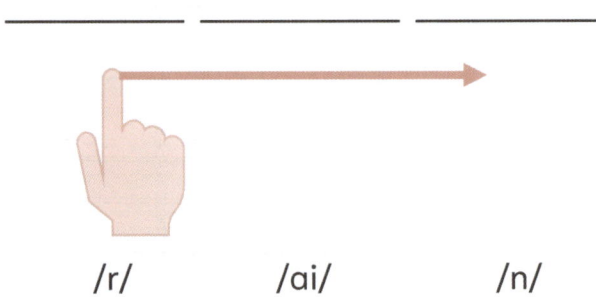

Using the VPM offer choices of what the first sound could be, e.g.

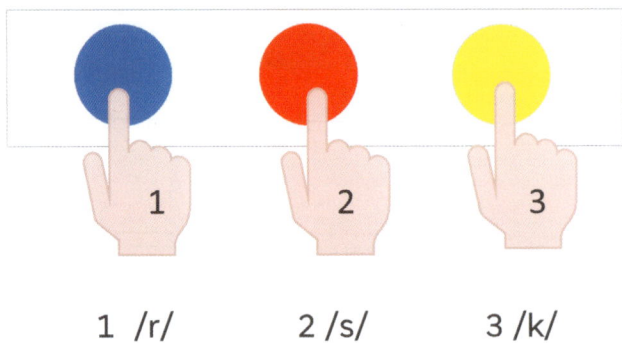

The child would point to the blue dot to indicate their choice as /r/ and can then be invited to write the letter on the first line.

This process is repeated for the next sound in the word, /ai/ represented by the grapheme ai, and then the last sound in the word, /n/ represented by the grapheme n, to complete the word.

There are a few things to consider when using VPMs for supporting both reading and spelling; these are randomisation and challenge.

Firstly, make sure that you randomise the position of the correct choice on the VPM so the child is not trying to spot a pattern in what you offer and is making choices on this basis.

Secondly, think about offering different levels of challenge.

You can do this by simply varying the number of items you offer. When first beginning to use this strategy, try just two options, moving on to three when the child understands the principle of how it works.

You can also vary the level of similarity of the items you present. For example, if asking the child to choose a sound, consider how similar your choices are. The sounds /n/ /t/ /s/ are distinctly different from each other, /v/ /z/ /m/ are less distinct and so offer a greater challenge and /m/ /n/ /r/ are similar offering the greatest challenge of all. If you are asking the child to choose a word: 'dog' 'can' 'hit' are very different, in that all the sounds in them are different, 'dan' 'did' 'dog' start with the same sound so this gives the child more to think about and 'dig' 'dog' 'dug' have only the middle vowel sound differing, so offering the greatest challenge.

You can build into your planning a gradual move towards offering a greater level of challenge for the child.

Offering choices on a VPM means that there is always a possibility that the child indicates correctly simply by chance. As it stands so far, they know that *one* of the options must be right so even if they're not sure, it's worth a guess. Reading and spelling is not about guessing, it is about accuracy.

So how can we get around this? A solution is to offer a 'this, that or something else' VPM. On this VPM there is a question mark instead of the final dot.

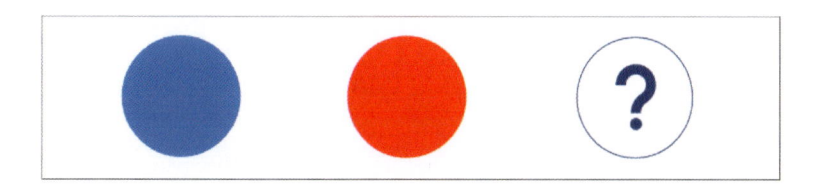

Imagine you are asking the child to read the word play. You offer 3 choices by pointing in the usual way *plate* (blue) *plane* (red) or *something else* (question mark). The correct choice hasn't been offered on either blue or red so the child must select 'something else'. You then present a new card (the conventional dot VPM) and offer more choices *pay* (blue) *pray* (red) *play* (yellow). In this case the child correctly chooses the yellow dot and the word play.

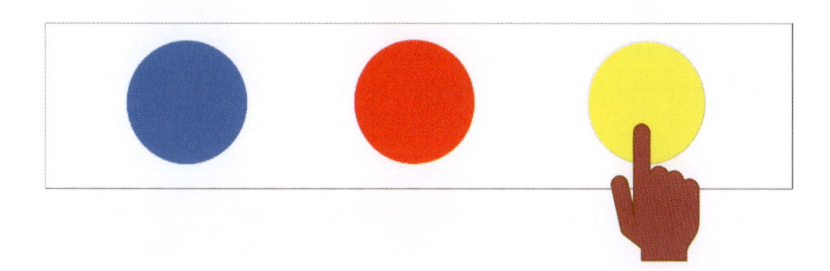

Visual place markers are included in the resources section in the Appendix at the end of this book.

b. **Matching Pictures to Single Words or Phrases**

A different strategy that can be used for reading words and phrases is picture matching. The child is shown a word or phrase to read and is offered a choice of pictures, only one of which matches. The child reads the word and points to the matching picture.

The reverse can also be used so the child is given a picture and a choice of words or phrases, only one of which matches. The child looks at the picture, reads all the words or phrases and points to the matching word or phrase.

For example:

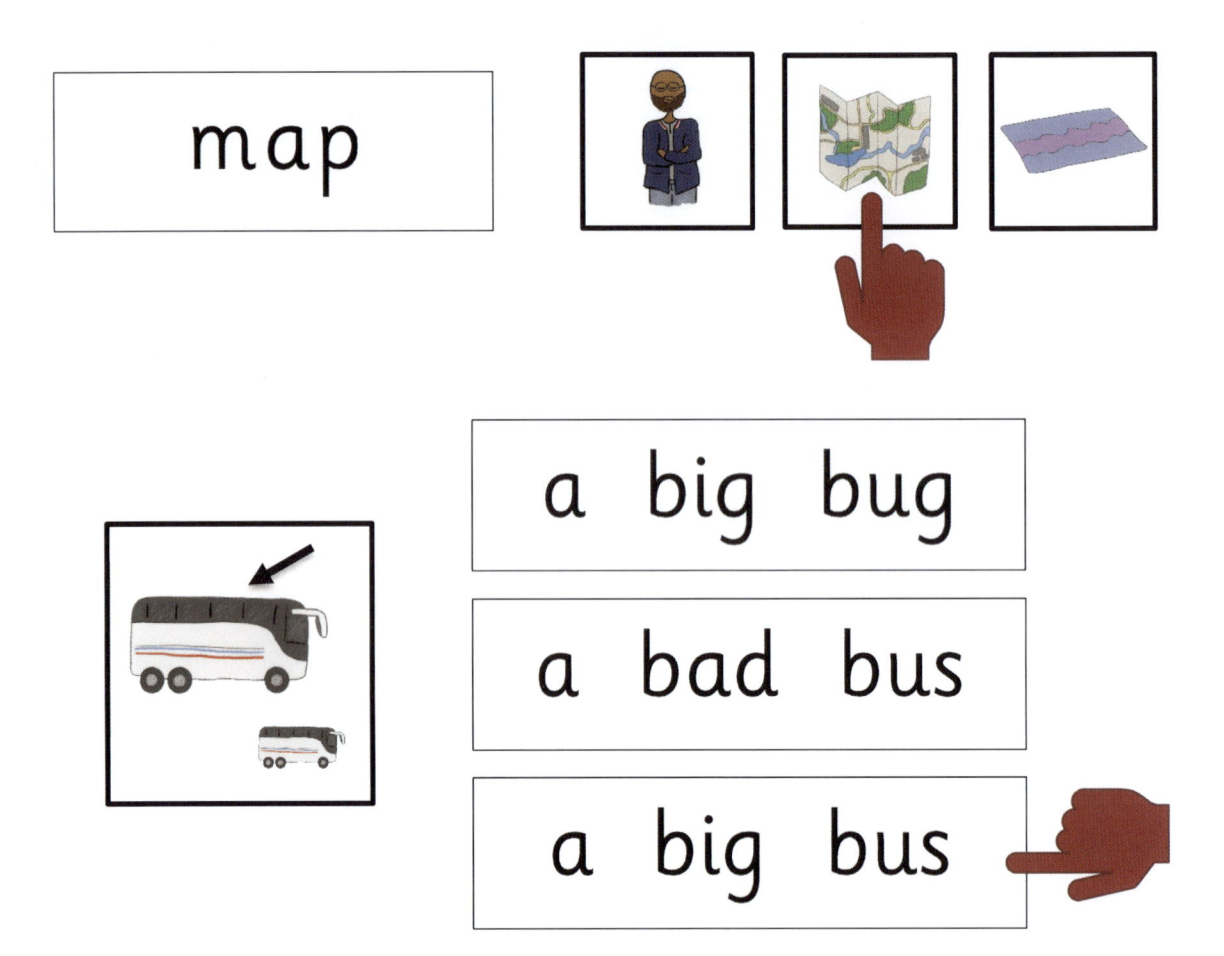

map

a big bug

a bad bus

a big bus

c. **Binary Responses Presented as Symbols**

In some situations, asking a child a closed question with a simple yes or no answer is useful. 'Yes' and 'no' symbol cards are a way of checking something quickly with a child.

In a similar way the 'good' and 'not good' cards can be used, particularly when reading and talking about and around the text.

These symbols are included in the resources section in the Appendix at the end of this book.

d. Number Cards

The number cards can be used when working on segmenting a spoken word into phonemes or when splitting a word into syllables.

The child can point to them in response to the question, "How many sounds can you hear in…?"

"How many sounds can you hear in the word stop?"

The child can point to them in response to the question, "How many syllables can you hear in…?"

"How many syllables can you hear in the word fantastic?"

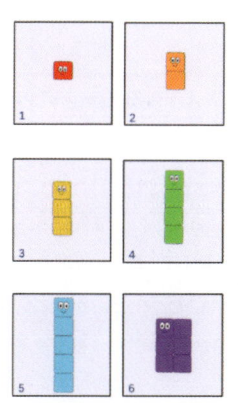

These symbols are included in the resources section in the Appendix at the end of this book.

e. Desktop Manipulatives

Desktop manipulatives can be just as useful for pre or nonverbal children as for children with physical disabilities. Being able to move things around to respond to a task avoids the need for a spoken response. Refer to the section on desktop manipulatives in the previous chapter for more information.

f. Big Oops!

'Big Oops!' is a very useful strategy to use with pre- and nonverbal pupils. The teacher reads or spells a word, phrase or sentence and randomly makes a mistake. When the child spots this, they point to the 'Big Oops!' card, the teacher stops and invites them to identify the error and help the teacher correct their mistake.

This strategy is useful for identifying what skills, concepts or knowledge the child has acquired.
Careful choice of the mistakes made can reinforce whatever we are currently working on or can focus on a specific area where the child needs more practise.

This symbol is included in the resources section in the Appendix at the end of this book.

g. Single Message Recording Devices

Single item recording devices, such as talking tiles or sound buttons, could be used to record information.

Pupils can listen to and remember the recordings and select the tile/button that has the sound, word or phrase required. It is important to ensure that the quality of recording is good enough to use in this way and note that set up can be time consuming and coverage may be limited.

An even more sophisticated solution is to use a Smoothtalker with a switch. The pupil uses the Smoothtalker choice progression capacity, listening to each of the options and making their selection by pressing the switch.

Telling Us What They Need

Pupils should also be given the opportunity to input into phonics lessons or 'have their say' when they need to. The 'I have something to say' card is a useful low-tech strategy that can be used for this. The large blue speech bubble indicates to the child that this is a way for them to give information. Symbol cards are placed in the speech bubble and the child can point to them to tell the teacher that they:

- want to work independently,
- need help,
- have made a mistake and wish to 'start again' to correct it.

Developing confidence and independence is very important for children with SEND, especially those with complex needs, who may experience little control over what happens to them during the day. The 'I have something to say' card should be available at all times in the lesson for the pupil to use.

Before beginning an activity, the pupil can indicate whether or not they feel they are able to do it independently by pointing to the 'I can do this by myself' card.

The pupil can also indicate that they need help whilst doing their work by pointing to the 'I need help, please' card e.g. when encountering a word they are not sure about when reading.

The request for help can be a little more specific using different symbol cards. If they need you to repeat information they point to the 'Say that again, please' card or if they want you to repeat a demonstration or action they can point to the 'Do that again, please' card.

They can also indicate they are aware that they have made a mistake and would like the opportunity to correct it by pointing to the 'Oops!' card.

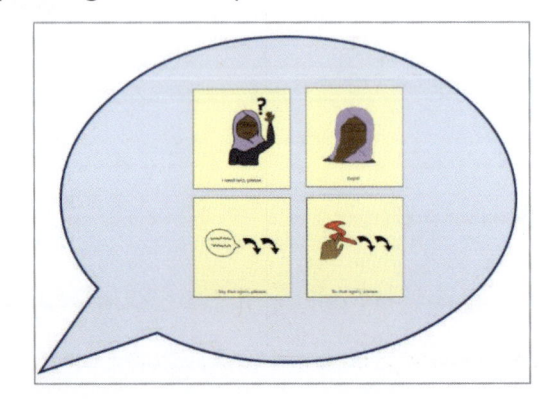

'I have something to say' card

As with any new strategy, introduce the 'I have something to say' cards gradually, starting with 'I need help, please'. The subtle difference between 'say it again' and 'do it again' can be introduced later as can 'I can do this by myself'.

These resources and symbols are included in the resources section in the Appendix at the end of this book.

Setting up the Teaching Environment

With all the tabletop card resources that are used with these pupils it is easy for the desk to get cluttered and disorganised which may be confusing for the child. For this reason, it is useful to centralise work on a single card so that the pupil knows where to look and what to focus on.

The 'My Work' card has a box at the top for a VPM and a box underneath for tabletop cards related to the activity e.g. word / phrase cards, worksheet snippets, number cards, Big Oops! etc.

'My Work' card

Don't forget to display the 'thinking voice' symbol so that you can refer to it and point to it throughout the lesson. The desk may look something like this:

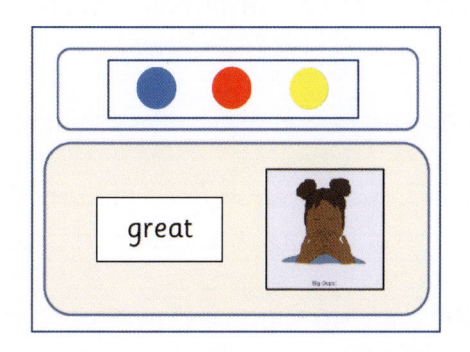

A range of resources, related to some of the strategies discussed, are available at the end of this book and may be photocopied for use in school. It is important that all learners see themselves in the books and resources we use. You will find a range of illustrations for each resource where a person is included, and the child can choose the one they feel is most appropriate for them.

Summary
- Encourage pre- and nonverbal pupils to use their 'thinking voice' in their head.
- Children should be able to give information about their learning and also information about what they need during lessons.
- Useful strategies for these pupils include:
    - Use of a visual place marker (VPM) to offer auditory choices.
    - Picture matching
    - Symbol cards
    - Desktop manipulatives

6. Access for Pupils with a Physical Disability who are Nonverbal

---

Pupils with physical disabilities who are also nonverbal are likely to have significant barriers to communication and access to the curriculum.

There is a powerful technology-based solution available to pupils that facilitates communication and supports access. This utilises the relatively simple strategy of monitoring an individual's eye movements, taking notice of where their eyes come to rest and how long they look at individual items such as a picture, symbol, letter/s or word. Prolonged attending to a specific item or 'dwelling gaze' on it, indicates interest and this can be used to indicate choice, if a selection of items is offered. This is known as 'Eye Gaze'.

There are numerous high-tech Eye Gaze technology systems available but using them in the context of phonics and reading instruction is not straightforward. A low-tech solution, the use of an Eye Transfer or E-Tran Frame, proves to be very flexible and effective.

An E-Tran frame is simply a rectangular sheet of clear Perspex with a central hole cut out. The frame can be held up between the pupil and the communication partner (teacher) so they can see each other clearly. Items can be placed on the frame and the teacher can see where the pupil looks and, more importantly, where their gaze dwells. Additionally, because of the central hole, the pupil can hear the teacher's voice clearly and see the lip patterns of their mouth.

Essentially, an E-Tran frame is used like a super-sized, vertical visual place marker with coloured dots placed around the frame, as below.

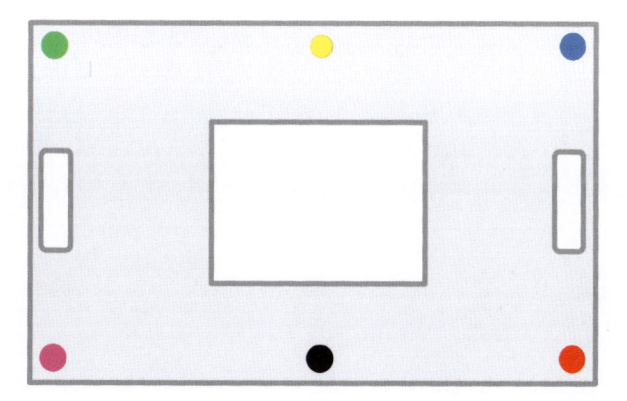

It works on a similar principle to a VPM but instead of *pointing* to make a selection, the pupil *looks at and dwells their gaze on* their chosen dot or item. The teacher can notice the 'dwell' and confirm the pupil's choice with them. Using the E-Tran frame in this way, both auditory *and* visual information can be anchored to dots and be offered as choices.

The frame has six coloured dots around the outside which act as the reference point for the pupil and teacher. Items such as pictures, symbols, graphemes, words or phrases can be stuck on the frame, each next to a dot, using Velcro, blue tac or nano tape. In the central space the 'I have something to say' cards can be placed on the frame so that the pupil can easily give additional information.

Using the Eye Transfer (E-Tran) Frame

The E-Tran frame enables pupils to respond to:
   a. a choice of **auditory** responses anchored to dots e.g. spoken sounds, words, phrases or sentences,
   b. a choice of **visual** responses anchored to dots e.g. written graphemes, words, phrases or sentences,
   c. matching pictures to single words or phrases,
   d. binary responses presented as symbols: yes / no *or* good / not good,
   e. number responses presented as symbols,

Here is a simple protocol for using the E-Tran frame for an activity:

- the teacher holds up the frame whilst sitting directly in front of the pupil,
- the pupil looks directly at the teacher (to indicate their selection is about to begin) and **initiates** the activity,
- *teacher verbally confirms that the selection is about to begin (optional),*
- pupil **scans** the items around the frame,
- pupil **dwells** their gaze on the chosen item,
- teacher **confirms** they recognize the choice by saying the colour of the dot that the item is near.

For example, the E-Tran frame is set up for a pupil to identify the word "cat" (spoken by the teacher) from a choice of three:

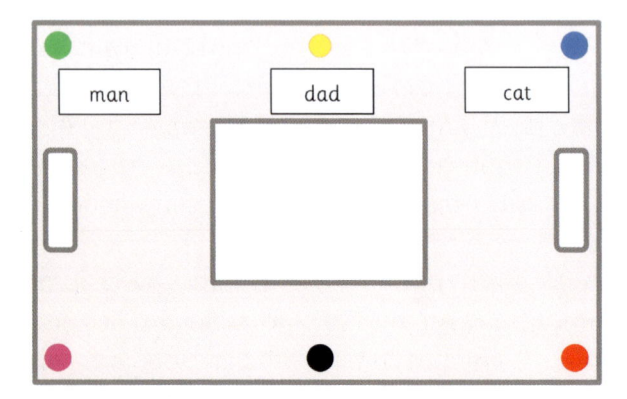

The child would look at the teacher through the frame then scan the words on it. They would then dwell their gaze on the blue dot. The teacher acknowledges this by saying blue and pointing to the card the child selected and talking about it.

This is a suggested protocol for pupils who do not usually use an E-Tran frame but who are using it for the purpose of accessing a reading and spelling programme.

These pupils are likely to need time to become accustomed to it and how to use it. It is recommended that before launching into the lessons the teacher and pupil are given time to practise using it by trialing basic (and importantly, fun) activities with pictures, to learn and practice the key skills of initiating, scanning, dwelling and confirming etc.

Advanced or able users of the frame may use a slightly different protocol. Instead of looking at the teacher and then scanning the items, they may dwell on a 'focus' spot on the frame to indicate that they are ready to start. This 'focus' spot is often, but not always, the yellow dot at the top. If this is the case, then the yellow dot is never used with a choice item. If pupils can manage this, then this is a much clearer signal of intent than simply looking at the teacher.

Some pupils may use an E-Tran frame as their everyday method of communication. For these pupils it is important to continue to use their familiar protocol which may or may not differ slightly from the ones above.

For phonics lessons, presentation will be similar to that described for in the activities in the previous chapter, just incorporating the frame, so please refer to that section. Please note that the majority, but not all strategies translate to use on an E-Tran frame and some extra notes have been added below:

a. When offering a choice of auditory responses anchored to dots e.g. spoken sounds, words, phrases or sentences,
    - select only 2-4 dots to anchor auditory information. Using the E-Tran frame to offer auditory information is much more challenging for the pupil than when offering visual information as there is no 'ever present' clue about auditory information once the teacher has finished speaking. The pupil is required to use a greater range of cognitive skills, including auditory memory, auditory sequential memory and working memory. Some pupils may have weaknesses in these areas, and it is important that the demands made on the pupil are an appropriate challenge, otherwise they may become disengaged. Use your professional judgment to decide to how many auditory choices are offered to the pupil using the E-Tran frame.
    - Place the 'or something else card', supplied, over the blue dot when employing this strategy e.g.

b. When offering a choice of visual responses anchored to dots e.g. written graphemes, words, phrases or sentences,
    - up to six choices can be offered. Use your professional judgment to decide to how many visual choices are offered, matching the number of choices to the pupil's needs.

c. When matching pictures to single words or phrases or vice versa,
    - The space above the central hole is a good place to position key resources with choices spread around the frame e.g.

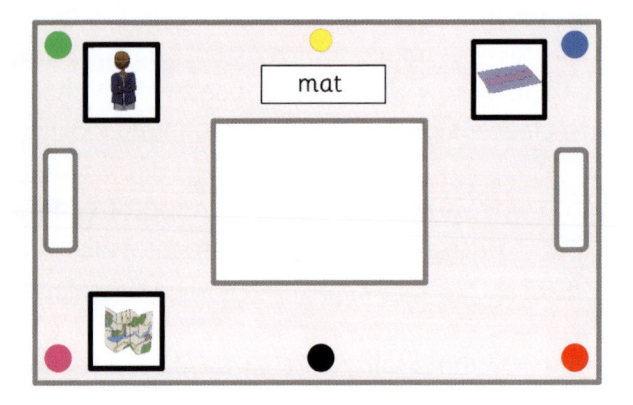

The 'I have something to say' symbols can be displayed to either side of the central hole, whatever the activity is.

Example of an activity with visual information anchored to dots:

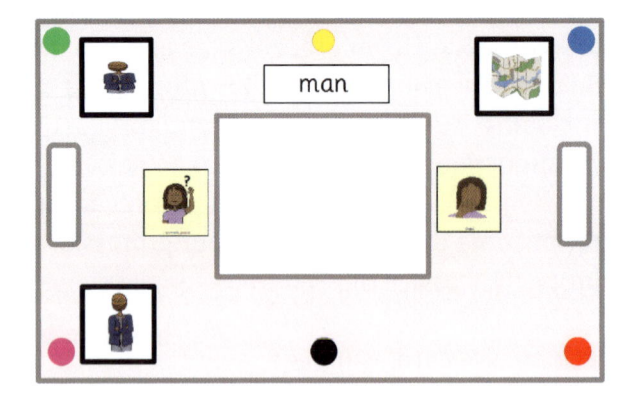

Example of an activity with auditory information anchored to dots:

Using an E-Tran Frame to Spell Words

The E-Tran frame can be used to spell out words using an established system that groups and colour codes letters that are anchored to dots on the frame. The same basic protocol is carried out when using the frame to select the sequence of letters to spell the word to the teacher. However, the following two steps are added to the protocol:

- pupil indicates which group the target letter is in by dwelling on the **group first,**
- teacher confirms this by stating the colour of the dot that the group is anchored to,
- pupil then dwells gaze on the **dot** that matches the colour of the letter in the group,
- teacher confirms this by stating the colour of the dot the pupil has indicated,
- teacher then says the **sound that matches the pupil's choice of letter.**

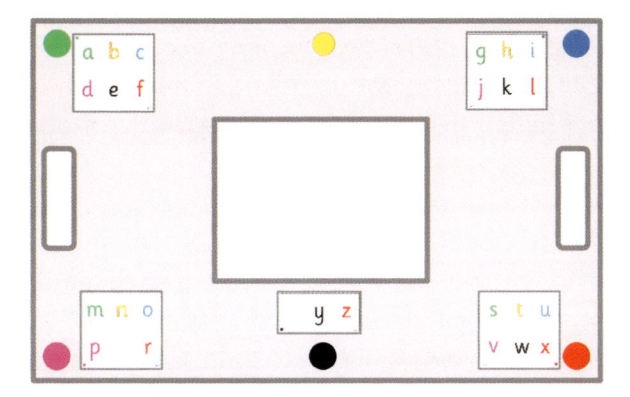

For example, a pupil working at basic code level wants to spell the word man:

The pupil dwells on the group in the bottom left (as they see it) which is anchored to the pink dot. They are choosing a letter that is within the group: m n o p r

The teacher confirms by saying 'pink'. The pupil then dwells on the green dot on the frame to choose the actual letter. The letter m within the m n o p r group is green so that is the choice of letter. Teacher confirms by saying 'green', the sound /m/ and writing the letter on a whiteboard.

So, when spelling the word cat, the protocol would be:

Group Green	Group Green	Group Red
Letter Blue	Letter Green	Letter Yellow
c	a	t

When a pupil first begins phonics instruction, sounds are introduced in an incremental progression. The graphemes on the E-Tran frame can be introduced gradually as well, following the progression of the phonics programme. There is a progression of E-Tran spelling cards available at the end of this book matched to sets 1-7 and qu in Book 3 of the Phonics for SEN programme.

Here is what the frame would look like working at the beginning of instruction:

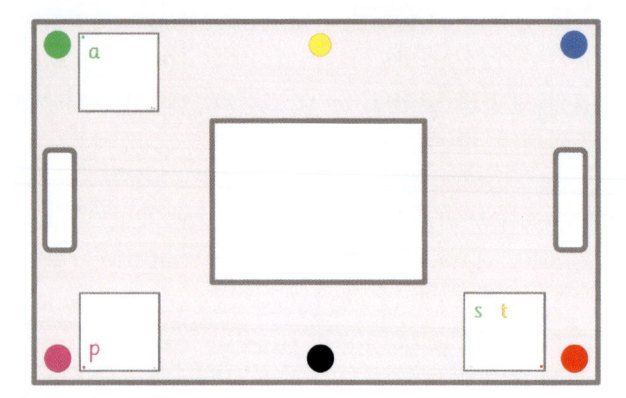

There are specific sets of cards for each of sets 1-7 of the Phonics for SEN programme which gradually build up the available letters.

Here is what the frame would look after working on **qu** in Book 3 of the Phonics for SEN programme:

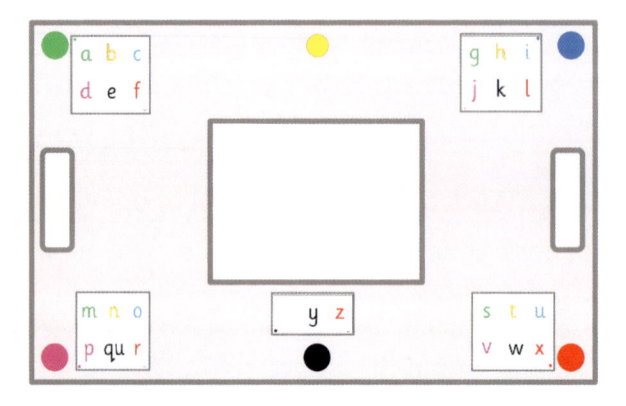

If the pupil is spelling a more complex word some of the graphemes may be made up of two or more letters. For these graphemes it is not appropriate to say the sounds (or indeed the letter names) for the component letters. If the pupil is spelling the word 'snow' with the sound spellings s n ow then the sounds are /s/ /n/ /oa/. When the pupil indicates the first letter of the grapheme for /oa/ **o** write it on the whiteboard for the pupil to see but say nothing. When the pupil indicates the second letter **w** write that next to the o on the whiteboard. At this point say the sound /oa/ and continue through the word.

> **Summary**
> - Useful strategies for these pupils include:
>   - Use of an E Tran frame to offer auditory choices
>   - Use of an E Tran frame to offer visual choices
>   - Picture matching
>   - Symbol cards

7. Access for Pupils with Sensory Needs

In the UK, pupils with sensory needs are supported by specialist teachers who have a mandatory qualification in their specific field.

Pupils with visual impairment (VI) are likely to be able to access phonics activities with appropriate adjustments to accommodate their needs. The child's VI teacher can provide information about their vision in a visual profile. The profile will also make recommendations on the use of strategies to support the learner: enlarging materials, using magnifiers, using steep sloping boards to position resources at eye level, as well as access to assistive technology such as a visualiser. Pupils with very low or no vision are likely to access braille, which is not covered in this book.

Pupils with hearing impairment (HI) are likely to be able to access phonics activities with appropriate adjustments to accommodate their needs. The National Deaf Children's Society has produced a document on teaching phonics to pupils with a hearing impairment[12]. The child's teacher of the deaf can provide information about their hearing in an auditory profile that includes the frequencies of sounds which are absent or indistinct.

Once aware of the pupil's auditory strengths and weaknesses you can make adjustments to how lessons are delivered. This includes:

a) incorporation of signing into lessons, if the pupil signs,
b) extended work on key sounds that are absent or indistinct (in the context of words, not in isolation),
c) the use of visual cues to highlight the presence of a sound, e.g. sound buttons, visual place marker strategies,
d) the use of Cued Articulation, a strategy developed by Jane Passy[11], supporting children with HI to notice sounds in words and to learn how to say the sounds accurately,
e) the inclusion of simple morphology activities once the pupil is secure with how the code works, e.g. exploring plurals to focus on /s/ at the end of words and 'ed' endings.

The profile also contains recommendations on the use of assistive technology to support the learner e.g. appropriate use of radio aids, sound field etc.

Children with multi-sensory impairments (MSI) have both a visual and hearing impairment. Specialist MSI teachers are able to give advice around managing the vision and hearing needs of these children and how to support communication and access to the curriculum. A combination of strategies will most likely be required.

Summary
- Children with sensory impairments are supported by specialist teachers who can give specific access advice via a visual or auditory profile.
- Children with VI, HI and MSI can access phonics if appropriate adaptations are made.

8. Access for Pupils with Other Needs

Sensory Processing

We are constantly aware of and processing information from the world around us and from our own bodies. Our senses detect these stimuli and neurological processes in the brain and literally 'make sense' of them enabling us to identify, understand, organise and respond to them appropriately and comfortably.

For some children this process is not straightforward. Difficulties in this area has been referred to as sensory processing disorder and it has been suggested to be a feature of autism and ADHD for some individuals.

Some children are noticeably over-responsive or under-responsive to these every-day stimuli and this can impact significantly on their interactions with the world around them. For example, children who are over-responsive may be sensitive to light, loud or specific sounds, the feel of specific materials and textiles or certain smells and tastes. Experiencing these may cause distress or anxiety so the child actively avoids experiences that include these stimuli. This may include disliking messy play, dislike of certain foods, avoiding eye contact, putting their hands over their ears and avoiding the presence of others. Difficulties managing stimuli can result in the child expressing their distress by crying, vocalising, pushing things away and running off (commonly referred to as a meltdown) or the reverse, becoming unresponsive (or shutting down).

Children who are under-responsive may not respond when their name is used, may give delayed responses or have low attention to the people and things around them. Some children seek out sensory stimuli by needing to touch and explore objects and people, putting things in their mouth, throwing things or vocalising.

As with many things, children do not fall neatly into just these two distinct categories and many exhibit a mixed profile of responses. Additionally, many children vary from day to day, hour to hour, minute to minute in terms of response.

The impact of sensory processing needs on learning and access to the curriculum is most apparent in terms of the child's ability (in that moment) to attend and focus.

Although sensory processing disorder is not listed in the International Classification of Diseases (ICD) system in the UK or the Diagnostic and Statistical Manual of Mental Disorders (DSM-5) in the US, it is increasingly common for NHS Occupational Therapists to assess children and provide a Sensory Profile for parents/carers and schools. This profile details a child's individual pattern of sensory processing, recommendations for creating a suitable environment and for enabling access to learning.

Before starting work with the child, the teacher makes sure that their sensory needs are being met so that they are in the best position to engage with any learning activity.

Processing Speed and Working Memory

The term 'processing' is used to describe how the brain perceives, organises, understands and responds to information. For some children with SEND their speed of processing is slower than that of their peers.

Working memory is the ability to keep information in our mind, monitor it and update it as new information is received. This information is used for learning and problem solving. Working memory capacity is limited by the amount of information individuals can hold in mind and for how long they can access it. For some children with SEND their working memory capacity is lower than that of their peers.

Both slow processing speed and low working memory capacity impact on a child's access to phonics and their rate of progress. For different reasons, these both impact on the following:

- maintaining focus and attention,
- ignoring distractions,
- following the progress of an explanation,
- following a series of instructions,
- completing tasks independently.

Impact on Attention and Focus

So, how do teachers manage the needs of these children and enable them to access phonics?

For any child who has limits to attention and focus there will be an impact on their capacity to engage in formal learning and a semi-formal approach may be beneficial. For these pupils the teacher plans phonics sessions in the usual way but the delivery is flexible and responsive to the pupil. Often these pupils will be supported by an additional member of staff in the classroom. Support staff become highly attuned to the child's emotional regulation and potential for engagement at any one time. When the member of staff notices that the pupil is in a position to engage with directed tasks, then they start to work through the planned activities, mindful that they need to monitor the pupil's attention and exit the session when the child appears anxious or restless. If the pupil is receptive to learning on more than one occasion during the day, then staff take the opportunity to deliver more directed learning. In special schools these pupils are likely to be in classes operating a semi-formal curriculum with thematic, meaningful and relevant activities planned across the day. Phonics instruction, as described above, is easy to incorporate into a semi-formal curriculum.

Pupils may benefit from the use of a visual timetable of the lesson that uses symbols, corresponding to the *types* of activities found in the programme. Before the lesson begins, the appropriate lesson symbols can be selected and placed on a timeline. Once the pupil has completed an activity it can be removed from the timeline so that the pupil is able to see how the lesson is progressing.

It must be stressed that not *all* pupils respond well to visual timetables.

The symbols used in a visual timetable can also be used as a basis for a plenary or review of learning at the end of the lesson or session. In the resources section at the end of this book there is a symbol board set out for a plenary, but this could be cut into individual symbol cards to make a timetable.

As well as considering the above aspects it is also important to remember the following when planning lessons for the complex pupil:

- provide a quiet environment that is not visually 'busy' to minimise distractions,
- when giving explanations make points singly and give the child time to process the information before moving onto the next point,
- when giving instructions break down a series into single instructions and give the child time to process the information before giving the next one,
- split larger tasks into smaller chunks,
- scaffold teaching, beginning with modeling and a gradual hand over of responsibility,
- offer lots of variety in lessons - activities should change frequently to maintain interest and engagement,
- time limit any one type of activity and keep them brief - remember that all the items in an activity or on a worksheet *don't have to be presented in one sitting* - they can be presented as snippets spread over a number of lessons,
- remember that this type of lesson is intense because of the frequency and length of pupil-teacher interactions – be aware that the pupil may tire so consider planning in a low intensity activity mid-way which gives the pupil an opportunity to rest,
- pupils with difficulties attending and focusing for sustained periods of time may benefit from carrying out clusters of activities spread out across the day rather than all in one sitting,
- pupils are likely to require teaching and learning opportunities presented at a slower rate of progression (in smaller steps) with much overlearning and repetition.

Summary
- Children with sensory processing needs can access phonics via a semi-formal delivery.
- Processing speed and working memory capacity impact on access to phonics activities.
- Children with these needs benefit from the use of visuals to support their learning.

9. Teaching Blending

Blending is the ability to join speech sounds (phonemes) together to make a meaningful word. Often this is described to children as 'pushing sounds together' so they can understand what happens when we blend.

Let's think about reading a simple word 'sat'. Commonly, children are taught to blend as follows:

"Look at the letters one by one and say the sounds that match:

$$s \quad a \quad t$$
$$\downarrow \quad \downarrow \quad \downarrow$$
$$/s/ \quad /a/ \quad /t/$$

then push the sounds together and say what that makes."

If asked, many children would not be able to say what this makes. To them, the teacher has said three separate things and got from those to a single thing – the word sat. It is almost like a magic trick. Let's consider what we are asking the child to do. They look at the first grapheme in the word, recall which sound it represents and says it either out loud or in their thinking voice in their head. Then they move onto the next grapheme, think of that matching sound then move onto the next and so on until they have worked through the word. Then they go back and recall the sequence of sounds they just said, and then they join those sounds to make the word. This process places a heavy emphasis on memory and processing skills which many of our pupils with SEND have difficulties with.

So, let's look at a subtly different way to approach this. This time, the teacher models actively or dynamically blending, like this: "Look at the first letter and say the sound that matches. Keep saying the sound while you look at the next letter and say the sound that matches that one.

$$s \; a \; t$$
$$\downarrow \; \downarrow \; \downarrow$$
$$> \quad >$$
$$/s/ \quad /a/ \quad /t/$$

"sssssaaaaa...

Note this is written to simulate what it might sound like.

Keep saying that sound while you look at the next letter and say the sound that matches that one.

s a t
↓ ↓ ↓
/s/ > /a/ > /t/

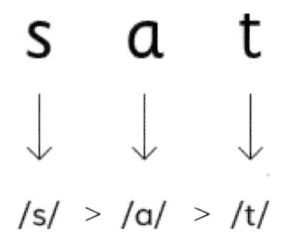

"ssssssaaaaat"

You have joined all the sounds as you move through the word, and just need to listen for the word forming."

"sat"

In this way each sound is picked up and connected to the next as the child tracks through the word, sounding like this, "sssaaat". We do need to acknowledge that we are kind of saying the word very slowly so we need to ask the child to think about what it would sound like at an ordinary speed.

Let's consider what we are asking the child to do now. Just like before they need look at the first grapheme in the word, recall which sound it represents and say it either out loud or in their thinking voice in their head. But this time they keep saying that sound until they are ready to say the next and so join the first sound to the next – they pick up each sound and run with them through the word. All the child has to do is listen to the word forming and says what they hear. The emphasis is less on memory and processing and more on listening. This is a much easier task, especially for pupils with SEND.

The technical term for this is connected phonation and it is the subject of an increasing amount of research with positive outcomes. A belt and braces approach is perhaps best when working with beginner readers, so utilising both of these strategies is recommended. When a child is required to read a word, we ask them to point to each grapheme in turn and say the matching sound. The go back to the start of the word and blend using the connected phonation technique, finally saying the word they heard forming.

So how do we teach our pupils to blend? Usually this goes something like this:

Stage 1: The teacher models a good blending technique for pupils, showing them what to do and so how to decode a given word.

Stage 2: The child tries the technique themselves with words matched to the phonics they are working on in class. The teacher provides lots of scaffolded activities for the pupils to practise and master the skill. An example of this is tandem blending (where teacher and pupil blend together with a gradual release of responsibility to the pupil).

Stage 3: The child blends independently but the teacher steps in to error correct and support as required.

Blending is not an easy skill to master and for many learners with complex needs even this heavily scaffolded approach doesn't enable them to find a way into blending. The 'A Place to Read' activity is helpful for these children as it introduces blending in a way that models a good technique and shares the load. In 'A Place to Read', the child focuses on one aspect of the process, listening for the word forming, and the teacher contributes by providing the connected phonemes. The child is prepared for reading with the sounds anchored to visual place markers and the whole activity tied into revealing the word.

The 'A Place to Read' activity is carried out as follows:

• Set out the appropriate 'A Place to Read' card in front of the child.

There are four cards in the Appendix section at the back of the book for working on words with 2,3 or 4 sounds.

• Choose a word that is matched to the phonics the child is working on in class and find a simple picture to represent it. Place this picture face down in the square on the card.

• Model dynamic blending by saying the sounds in the word and pushing them together as you go. As you do this point to the visual place markers on the card (green dots). Make sure that you are pointing to the dot that corresponds to the sound you are saying within the word. Your finger will move across and through the dots as you speak.

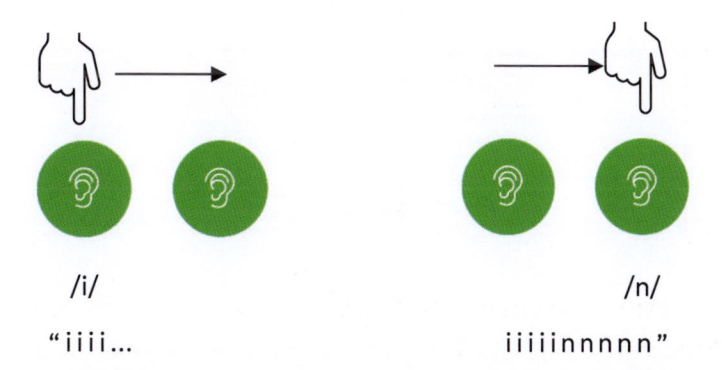

/i/   /n/

"iiii...   iiiiinnnnn"

When you have said the last sound in the word, without saying anything else (because that would be distracting), tap the space after the word.

Soon this 'tap' will become a signal for the child to say the word they heard forming, but this may need some explanation at first.

• When the child says the word, turn over the picture card so they can see if they are right and talk about the word.

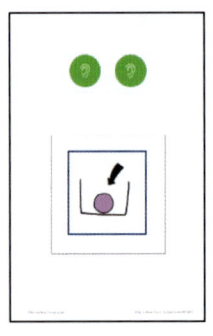

When modelling blending, it is important to consider the type of sounds in the word you have chosen. Sounds vary in quality depending on how they are articulated and as a result some are easier than others to blend. Continuant sounds such as /s/ /f/ /l/ /r/ /m/ and /n/ are easy to blend because it is possible to extend them to some extent, giving the child time to look at the next grapheme and say what it is as part of the blending process. When children are first learning to blend it is helpful to focus on these continuant sounds and gradually incorporate the sounds that are more difficult to articulate, such as /b/ /d/ /g/ /t/. When blending these sounds, it is important to model and later make sure that the child moves briskly on from these sounds to the next.

Move pupils on from A Place to Read to conventional word-based blending activities as soon as the child is able.

Summary
- Blending is taught using teacher modelling and scaffolded activities.
- Dynamic blending (continuous phonation) makes blending accessible.
- The A Place to Read activity is a way into blending for children with complex needs.

10. Teaching Segmenting

Segmenting is the ability to split up spoken words into their constituent phonemes in sequence. Following on from this a grapheme can be assigned to each sound and so the word is spelled.

Commonly, children are taught to segment by identifying initial sounds in words, then after a while identifying the final sound in words and then the middle sound in words. Phoneme frames are used where the child segments the word and pushes counters into boxes as they say each sound. Segmenting a spoken word is a sequential process, accessing and isolating individual sounds one by one through the word.

As with blending, segmenting is not an easy skill to master and for many learners with complex needs we need to find a way into segmenting. The 'A Place to Listen' activity is helpful as it introduces segmenting in a way that models a good sequential technique and heavily scaffolds the process. Once again, the sounds are anchored to visual place markers.

The 'A Place to Listen' activity is carried out as follows:

• Set out an appropriate 'A Place to Listen' card in front of the child.

Note that there are two cards with dots on for VC words and three cards with dots on for CVC words. The position of the red dot on the card indicates the position of the target sound in the activity. Cards are found in the Appendix section at the back of the book.

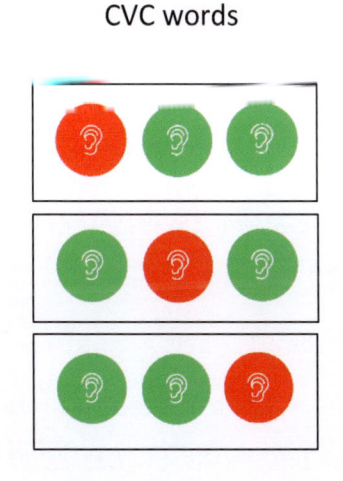

VC words   CVC words

• Choose a word that is matched to the phonics the child is working on in class and find a simple picture to represent it. Place this picture face up next to the card to serve as a visual prompt to remind the child what the word is.

• Let's work on the word 'run'.

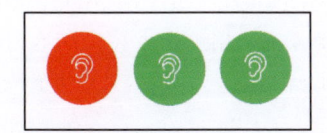

51

Begin by pointing at the red dot and ask the question, "What sound can you hear, here in the word run?" As you say the word move your finger left to right across the dots so that the sounds correspond to the dots as you say them in the word, i.e. saying the word as if dynamically blending.

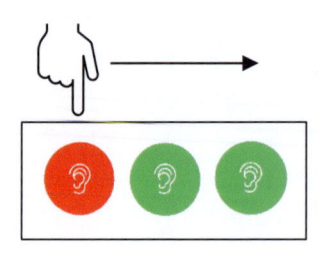

"rrrrrruuuuunnnnn"

Note this is written to simulate what it might sound like.

- You may have to repeat this several times before the child is able to identify the sound. If they find it difficult to identify the sound, allow your finger to linger on the red target sound dot and emphasise the sound slightly so it is easier to isolate.

- Notice the language used in this activity, "What sound can you hear, *here* in the word...?" The child is not asked what the first / initial / beginning sound is. The dot acts as a visual place marker and pointing directs the child to *where* in the word to listen. This avoids use of any vocabulary that the child may not know securely such as ordinal or positional language. The same question can be used wherever the target sound is positioned.

- The child is not required to write or match a sound spelling; this activity is purely aural and oral. At first the child will need lots of experience and practise to be able to consistently identify the initial sound in lots of different words. Once the child is confidently identifying the initial sound then move on to the middle sound using the same technique and the appropriate card. Similarly, once the child is confident in identifying the middle sound then move on to the final sound using the same technique and the appropriate card. In this way the child works through words in the sequence they will come to rely on when they are using the technique for spelling words.

Move pupils on from A Place to Listen to conventional word-based segmenting activities as soon as they are able.

> **Summary**
> - Segmenting is taught using teacher modelling and scaffolded activities.
> - Segmenting a word involves sequential isolation of sounds.
> - The A Place to Listen activity is a way into segmenting for children with complex needs.

11. Listening to a Child Read

Listening to a child read is an important part of reading instruction for all children. Whether they are reading a story, a poem, or a non-fiction text, they can immerse themselves in all that it offers and have the satisfaction of reading it themselves.

This activity is important, not just for decoding practice, but also for reasons related to all the other aspects of reading, as described in Scarborough's Reading Rope. Remember, 'We Teach the Rope'.

If we focus on decoding the text though, we can see that listening to a child read is an opportunity to assess their decoding accuracy. When the child makes a mistake, it's an opportunity to step in and intervene to correct any errors, provide them with any knowledge they lack and support them with blending. Listening to a child read like this, therefore, is a component of instruction.

All beginner and developing readers benefit from access to phonically controlled books (decodable readers) that match to the phonics they are working on in class. These not only give the child the opportunity to apply the phonics they have been learning to read text, but they also build their confidence and enjoyment of reading. These books can be phased out as children move through their phonics programme and have enough knowledge of the code to tackle any text of their choosing.

These are some of the decodable readers that accompany the Phonics for SEN programme.

Listening to a child read also gives us an opportunity to ask them questions and promote discussion about the text they have read, further stimulating interest and enabling us to look into their reading comprehension.

In lessons we model fluency by reading with pace and prosody and we can have the child read and re-read along with us or with peers.

However, all this is dependent on the child being able to read the text aloud to the teacher. This isn't an option for pre and nonverbal children.

Children who are verbal can read, or attempt to read, every word on the page. Theoretically, this is also possible for a child who is nonverbal if the teacher stops after each and every word and uses, for example, a VPM or E-Tran frame to offer auditory choices. This is a thorough but not very satisfactory approach to take to reading an entire text as it will impact significantly on the flow of reading and, importantly, the child's enjoyment and engagement. This is not something to be recommended! It is far better to use a range of strategies within a single reading session with the use of a VPM or E-Tran frame included in sensible measure.

Many of the access strategies discussed and explained in this book can be used when asking the child to read a book and below are some suggestions for their application:

- the use of a VPM or an E-Tran frame to read selected single words, e.g. an isolated word, a word within a sentence (with the teacher reading the other words)
- the use of a VPM or an E-Tran frame to read phrases or whole sentences within the text,
- modelled reading, where the teacher reads the text, indicating every word by pointing and moving the finger 'through the word', checking the child is following,
- shared reading, where teacher and child take it in turns to read sentences in a text,
- modelled reading with Big Oops!, where the teacher reads the text, indicating every word by pointing and moving the finger 'through the word' but makes a deliberate mistake for the child to spot (not appropriate for an E-Tran frame),
- reading 'together', where the child is encouraged to 'read along' with the teacher in their 'thinking voice',
- the use of questioning to check accuracy:
  - ask the child to indicate if there are any words that they were not sure of and support to read, as required,
  - ask the child to read a particular word or phrase in a sentence they have just read (offer choices on a VPM or an E-Tran frame),
  - ask the child to point to a particular word or identify all the words in a phrase in a sentence they have just read,
  - ask the child a simple question related to the literal meaning of a sentence they have just read (offer choices on a VPM or an E-Tran frame),
- the use of questioning to work on reading comprehension and explore the text:
  - ask the child open questions about the text (offer choices on a VPM or an E-Tran frame),
  - ask the child questions that require them to draw inference and reach conclusions about the text (offer choices on a VPM or an E-Tran frame),
  - on completing the book, ask the child to sequence a series of pictures that relate to the progression of the story or information,
  - on completing the book, ask the child to draw something related to the text.
- the use of the yes / no symbols to quickly answer closed questions,
- the use of good / not good symbols to respond to simple questions about the action of characters, the plot progression and their thoughts on the book.

Offering a pick-and-mix approach is recommended to keep the child's interest, motivation and engagement high.

There are two inevitabilities we should be aware of that present themselves when working with pre- or nonverbal children in this situation.

Firstly, unless the child is at the very beginning of instruction, we have to accept that we cannot check reading accuracy for every single word in a book. We have to be flexible and accept that there will be some words, phrases or sentences that either we read for the child, or they are asked to read, and we assume they have done so with accuracy. As teachers, this can be a little unnerving, but the cost is outweighed by the benefits if the child is having a meaningful and enjoyable experience of reading or part reading a book. We have to consider the bigger picture and view each experience as contributing to the child's reading development.

The second inevitability is that using access strategies will slow down the rate of reading. Quite simply, it will take longer to read a book, even simple ones at the beginning instruction. The number of texts a child will get through at any one stage in phonics instruction may be significantly smaller than that of their peers. Potentially this sets up not just a 'decoding experience' gap but also a language gap as the child is not exposed to as wide a range of texts as their peers. This is why it is so important to make time to read a range of books **to the child**, alongside phonics instruction, so that they have lots of experiences of books and the language / imagery within.

> **Summary**
> - It is possible to 'listen' to a pre- or nonverbal child read using access strategies.
> - A pick-and-mix approach is best to keep interest and engagement high.
> - We have to accept that there are costs as well as benefits when structuring this activity with pre- and nonverbal children.

12. Summary

"Teaching children to read is a fundamental moral obligation of society."

Garrison Keillor
(via Prof Mark Seidenberg)[12]

At the beginning of this book, we considered a number of questions that are commonly asked around teaching pupils with complex needs to read and spell.

In this book we looked at the 'what' and the 'how' for these pupils.

What? What do we teach our pupils with complex needs?

It is clear from the research evidence how the brain learns to read and this points us towards systematic phonics instruction, with words synthesised from phonemes and graphemes. Linguistic phonics and traditional synthetic phonics programmes offer this type of instruction.

We still have several hurdles to climb for our learners with complex needs. There are persistent and unhelpful myths circulating in schools, but the guidance from the DfE points the way for improved practice and outcomes.

How? How do we teach our pupils with complex needs?

By far the biggest challenge is making phonics *accessible* to pupils with complex needs. In this book we explored simple strategies to use with these pupils and the resources for these are provided in the Appendix.

References

1. The reading framework: teaching the foundations of literacy - Guidance for schools to meet existing expectations for teaching early reading, Department for Education July 2021 Updated Jan 2022
2. National Reading Panel 2000, Teaching Children to Read An Evidence-Based Assessment of the Scientific Research Literature on Reading and Its Implications for Reading Instruction
3. Independent review of the teaching of early reading 2006, Jim Rose Dept for Education and Skills
4. Gough, P.B. & Tunmer, W.E. (1986). Decoding, reading, and reading disability. Remedial and Special Education, 7, 6–10.
5. National Reading Panel. A Closer Look at the Five Essential Components of Effective Reading Instruction: A Review of Scientifically Based Reading Research for Teachers. US Dept of Ed, 2004 Learning Point Associates, 2004
6. Moats, L. C., & Tolman, C. (2019). LETRS: Language essentials for teachers of reading and spelling (3rd ed.). Dallas, TX: Voyager Sopris Learning.
7. Scarborough, H.S. (2001). Connecting early language and literacy to later reading (dis)abilities: Evidence, theory, and practice. In S.B. Neuman & D.K. Dickinson (Eds), Handbook of early literacy research (Vol. 1, pp. 97-110). New York, NY: Guildford
8. Willingham D T, Hughes E M and Dobolyi D G (2015) The Scientific Status of Learning Styles Theories *Teaching of Psychology* 42(3):266-271
9. Ehri L C (2013) Orthographic Mapping in the Acquisition of Sight Word Reading, Spelling Memory, and Vocabulary Learning *Scientific Studies of Reading* 18(1), 5-21
10. Share D L (1995) Phonological Recoding and Self-Teaching: sine qua non of sine acquisition *Cognition* 55(2), 151-218
11. Wiley RW, Rapp B (2021) The effects of handwriting experience on literacy learning *Psychological Science* 32(7)
12. Rainbow Speakers (2022): Available from Discover Inclusion https://www.discoverinclusion.co.uk/rainbow-speakers
13. National Deaf Children's Society (NDCS) https://www.ndcs.org.uk/documents-and-resources/teaching-phonics-to-deaf-children-guidance-for-teachers/
14. Cued Articulation. Jane Passy, ACER Press Revised Edition 2010
15. Language at the Speed of Sight, Prof M Seidenberg. Basic Books 2017

Appendix

thinking voice	thinking voice
thinking voice	thinking voice
thinking voice	thinking voice

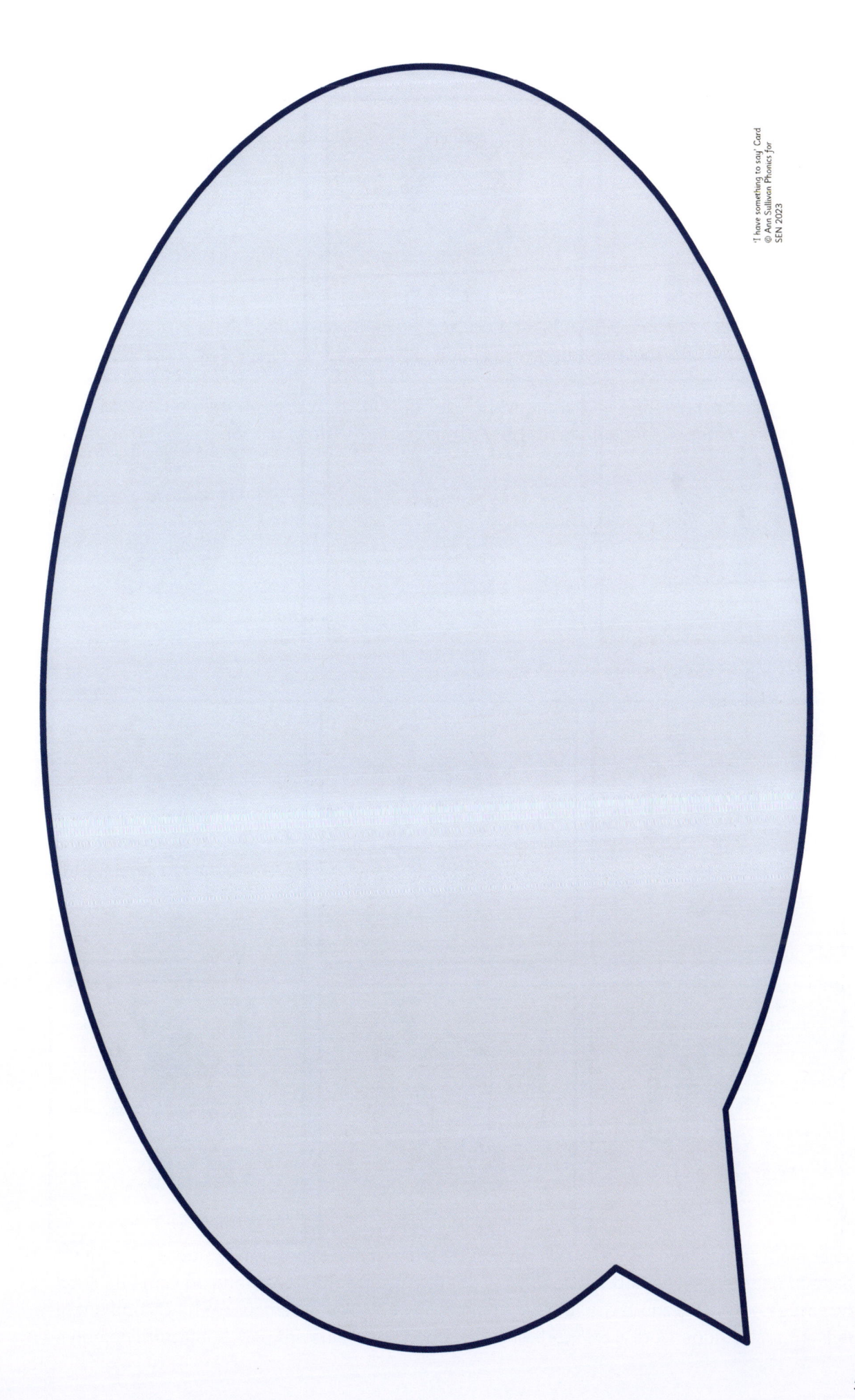

'I have something to say' Card
© Ann Sullivan Phonics for SEN 2023

'I can do this by myself' Symbol

I can do this by myself.	I can do this by myself.	I can do this by myself.
I can do this by myself.	I can do this by myself.	I can do this by myself.

'I need help please' Symbol

I need help, please.	I need help, please.	I need help, please.
I need help, please.	I need help, please.	I need help, please.

'Oops!' Symbol

Oops!	Oops!	Oops!
Oops!	Oops!	Oops!

'Do that or say that again' Symbol

Do that again, please.	Do that again, please.	Do that again, please.
Do that again, please.	Say that again, please.	

'My Work' Card © Ann Sullivan Phonics for SEN 2023

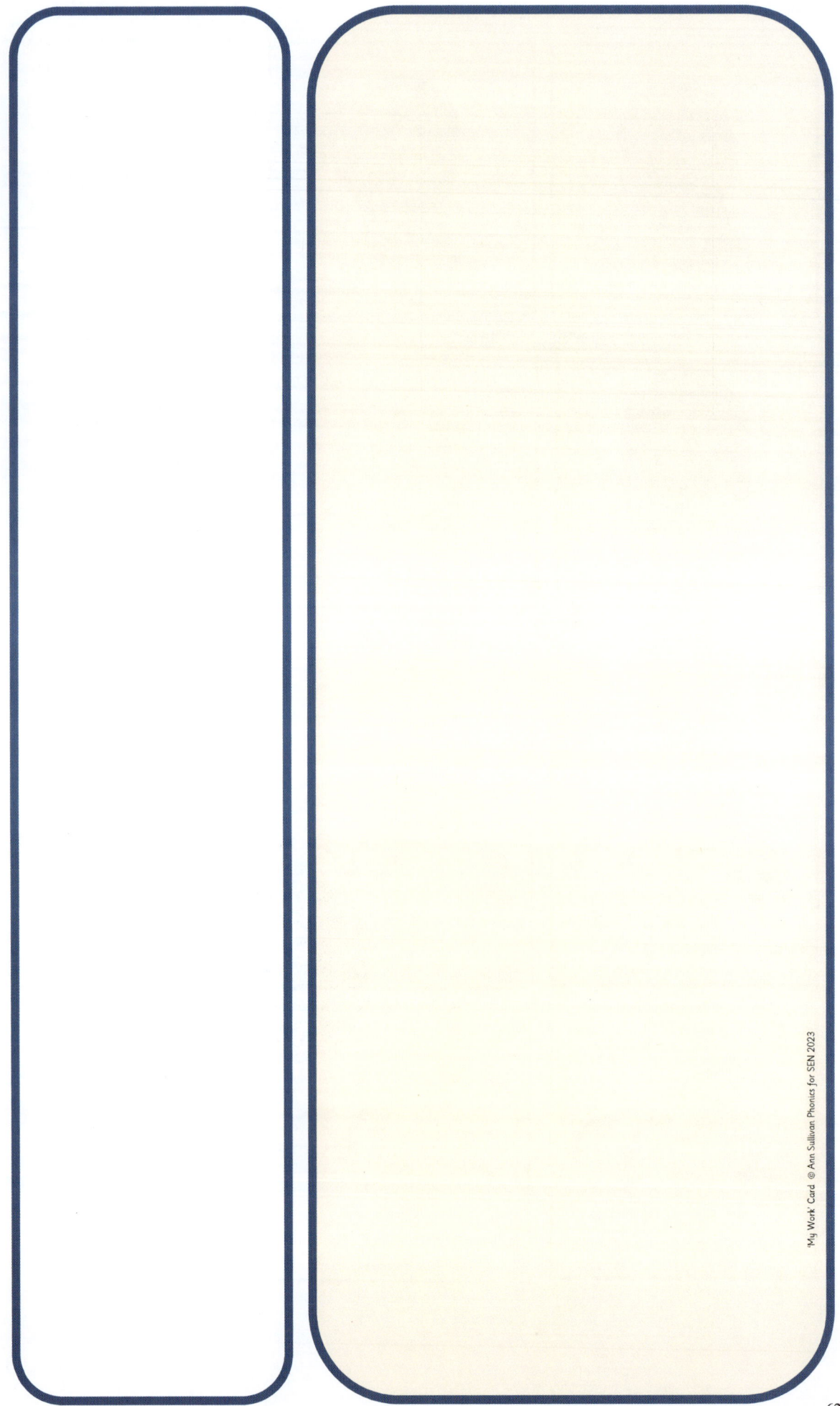

Visual Place Markers

Visual Place Marker and 'Big Oops!' Symbol

Big Oops!

64

Number Cards

1

2

3

4

5

6

65

Yes/No and Good/Not Good Cards

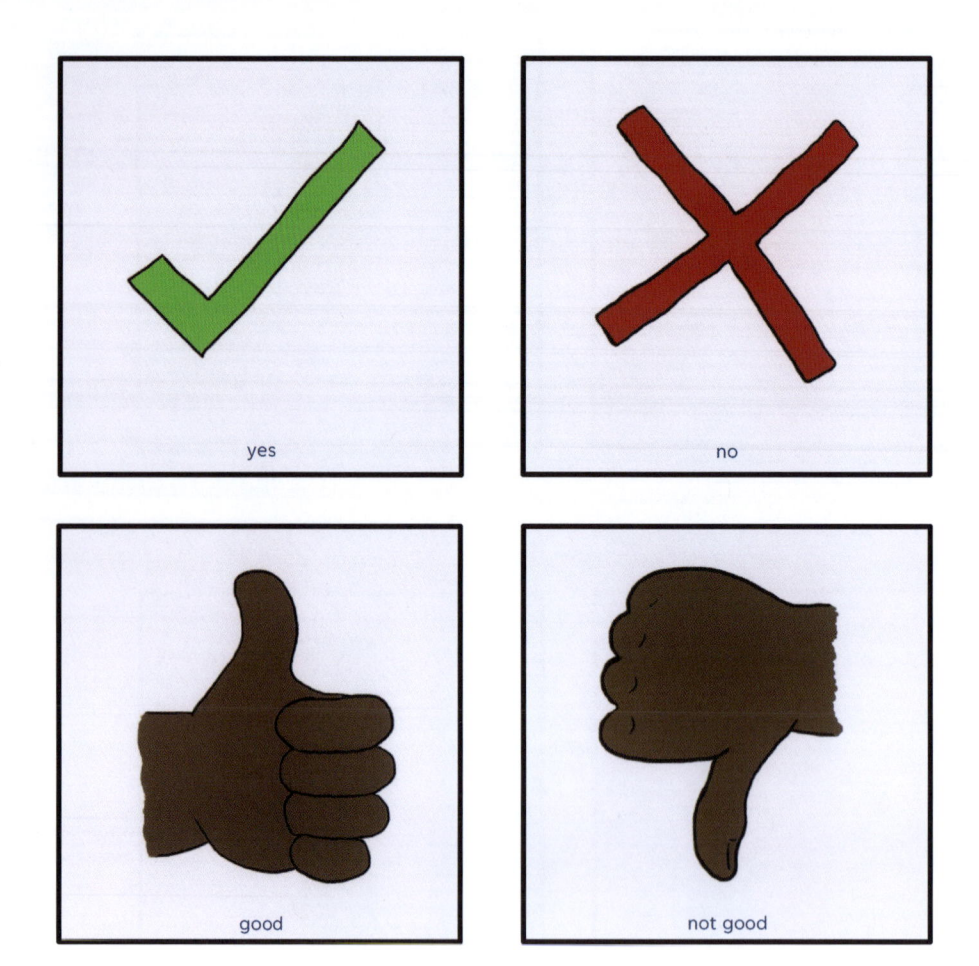

yes

no

good

not good

Plenary Card and/or Visual Timetable Symbols

sound or sounds	sound spellings / graphemes	blending
segmenting	Today's work	reading words
spelling words	sentences	reading a book

67

E-Tran Frame Cards

E-Tran 'Something else' Card

?

E Tran – Spelling Cards Set 1
dot on the card indicates which dot on the frame the card is placed near

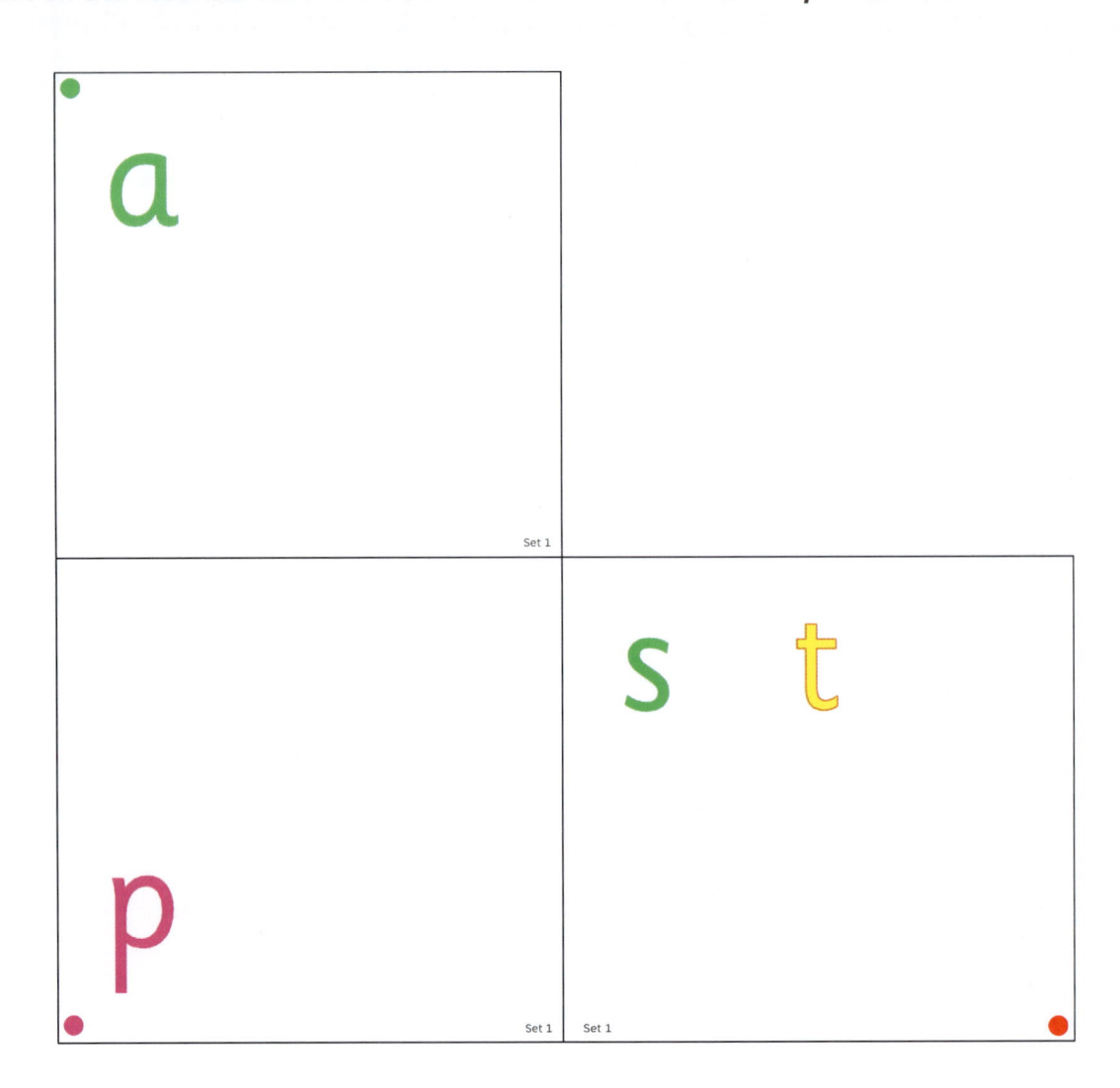

● a

Set 1

p

Set 1

s t

Set 1

68

E Tran – Spelling Cards Set 2

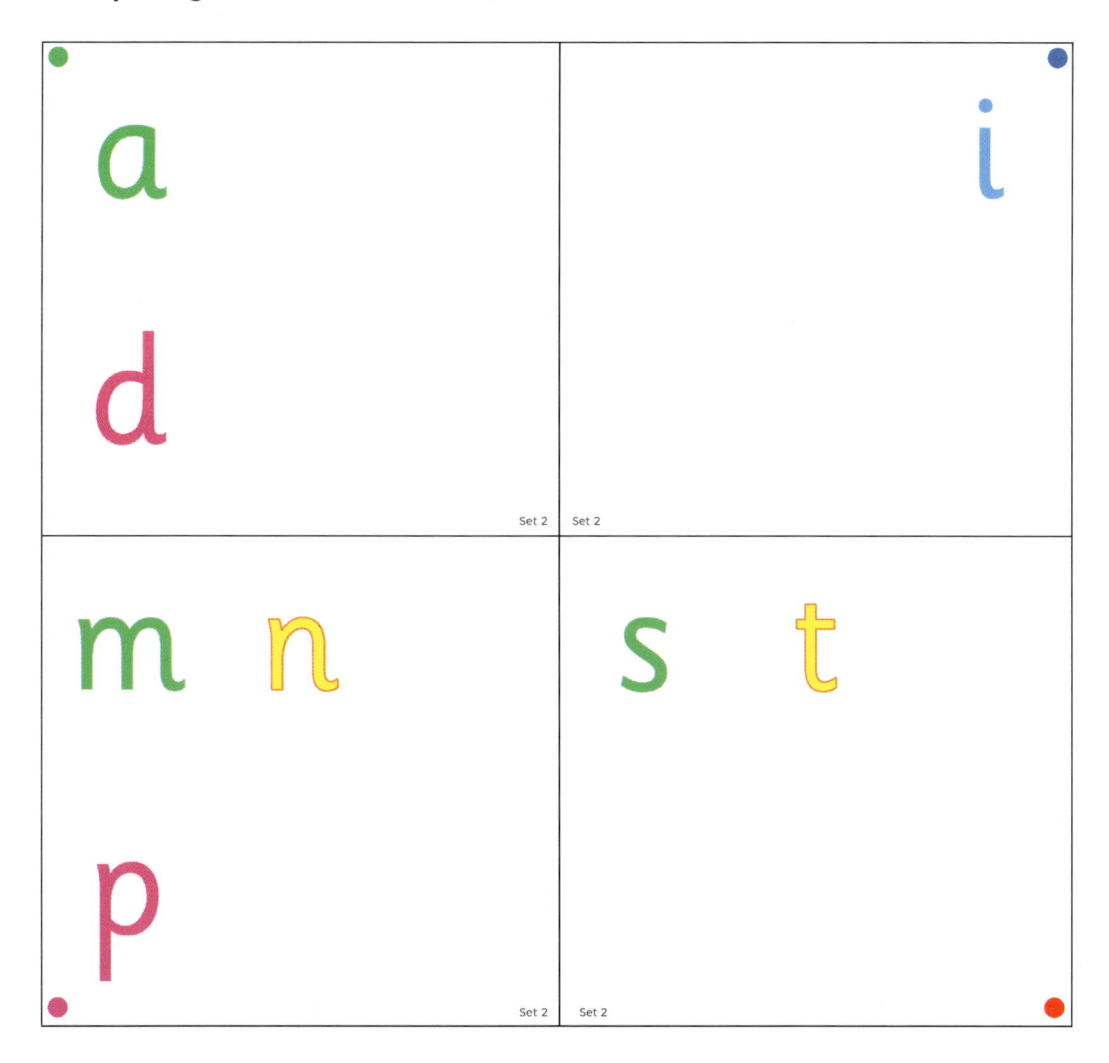

a	i
d	
m n	s t
p	

E Tran – Spelling Cards Set 3

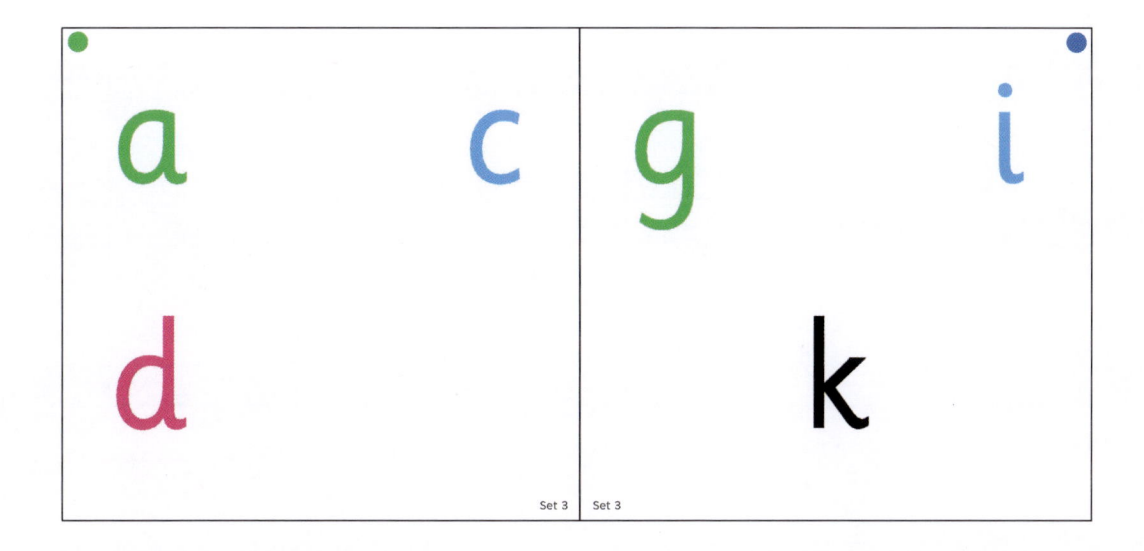

a c	g i
d	k

m n o   s t
p
Set 3   Set 3

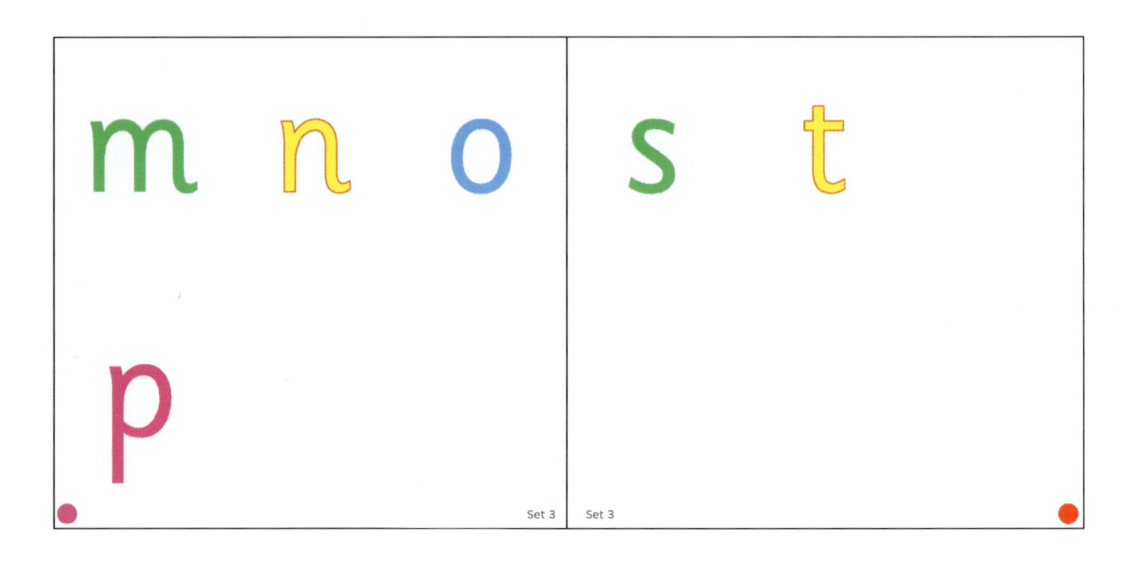

E-Tran Spelling Cards Set 4

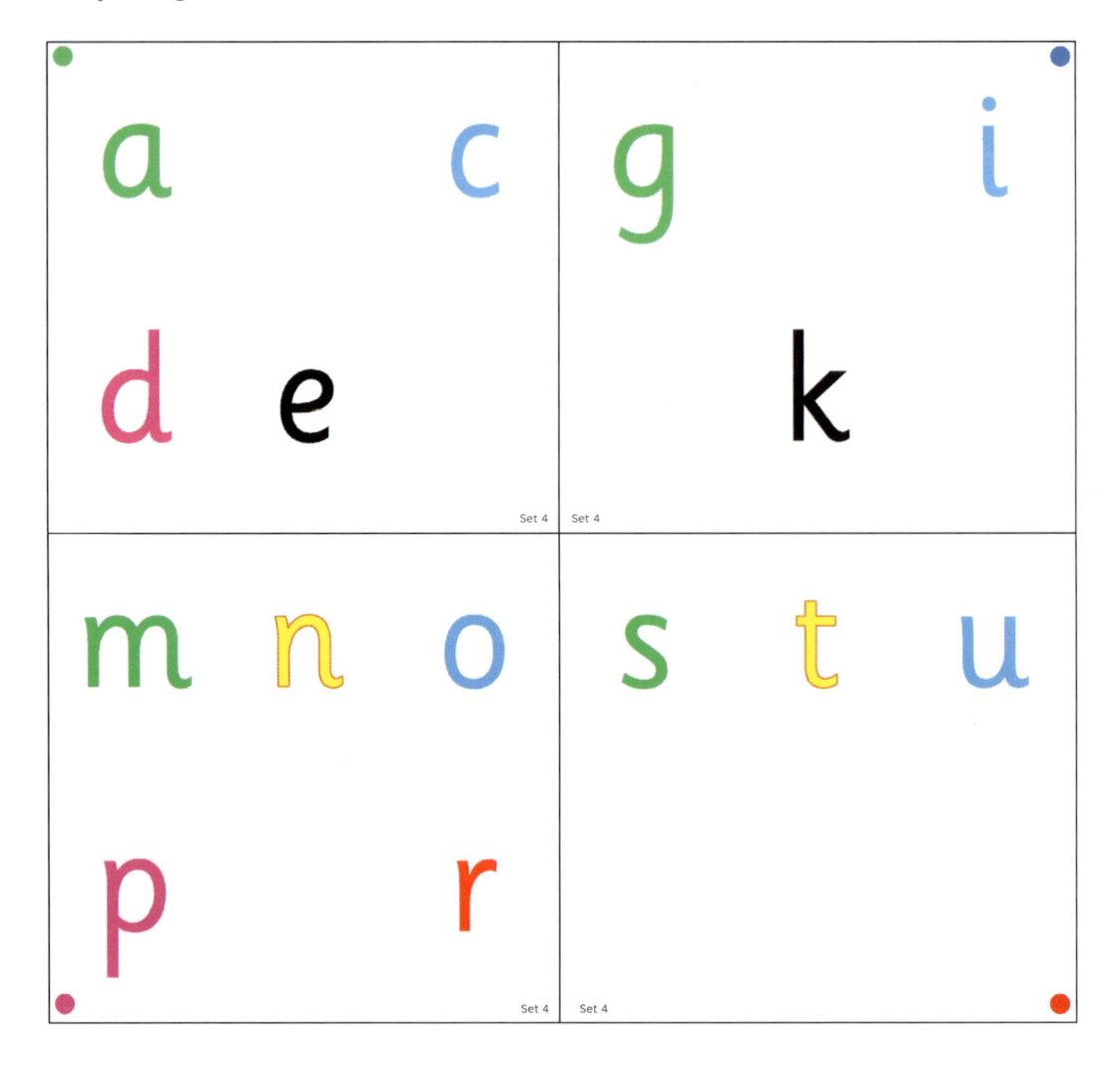

a c   g i
d e   k
Set 4   Set 4

m n o   s t u
p r
Set 4   Set 4

70

E Tran – Spelling Cards Set 5

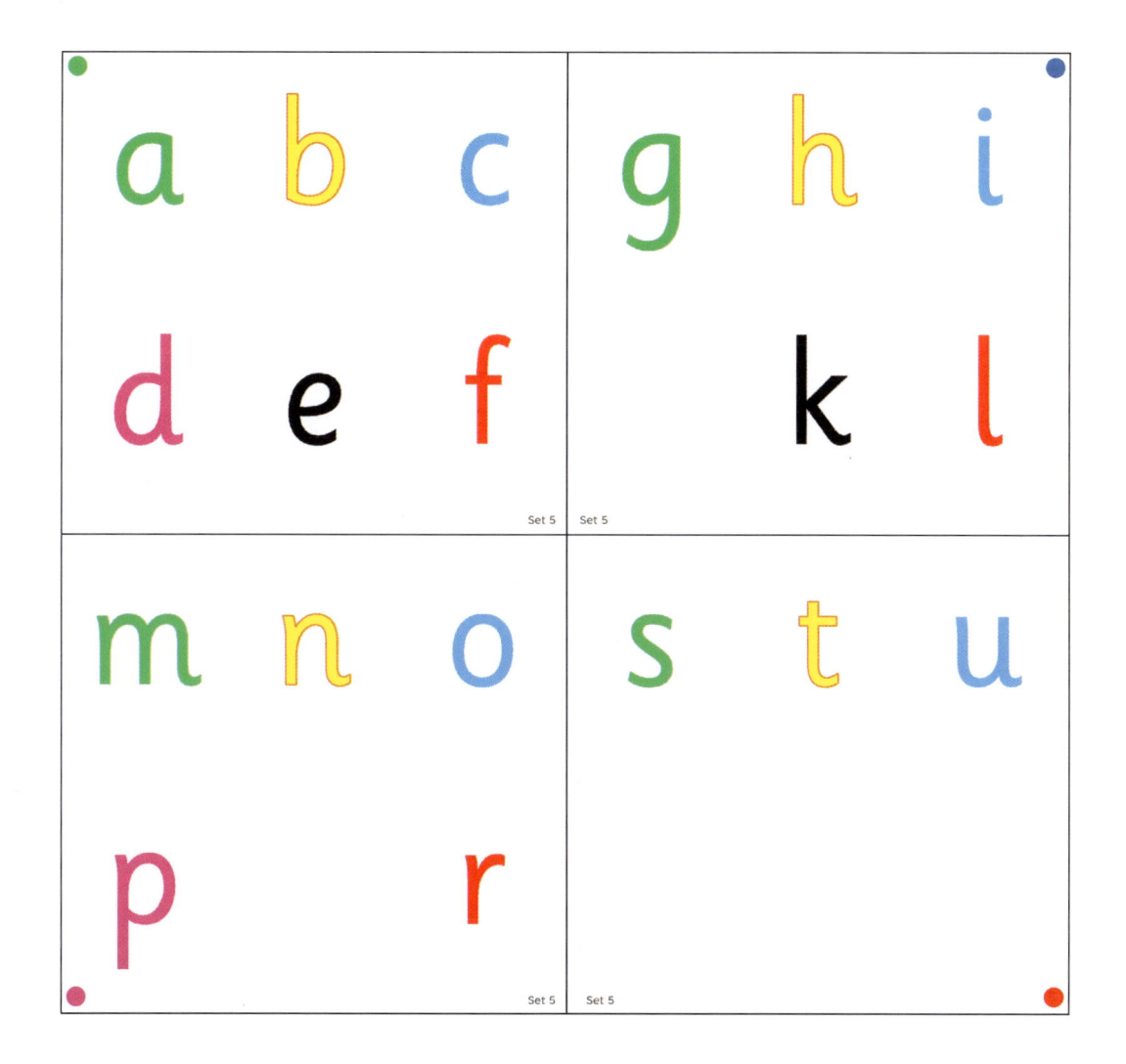

a b c	g h i
d e f	k l
m n o	s t u
p r	

E Tran – Spelling Cards Set 6

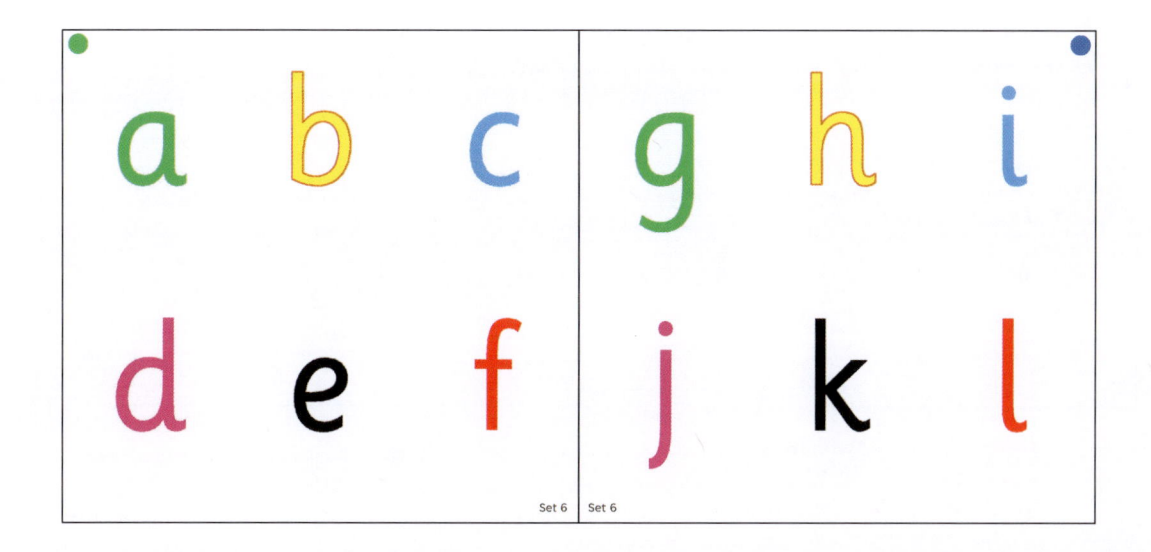

a b c	g h i
d e f	j k l

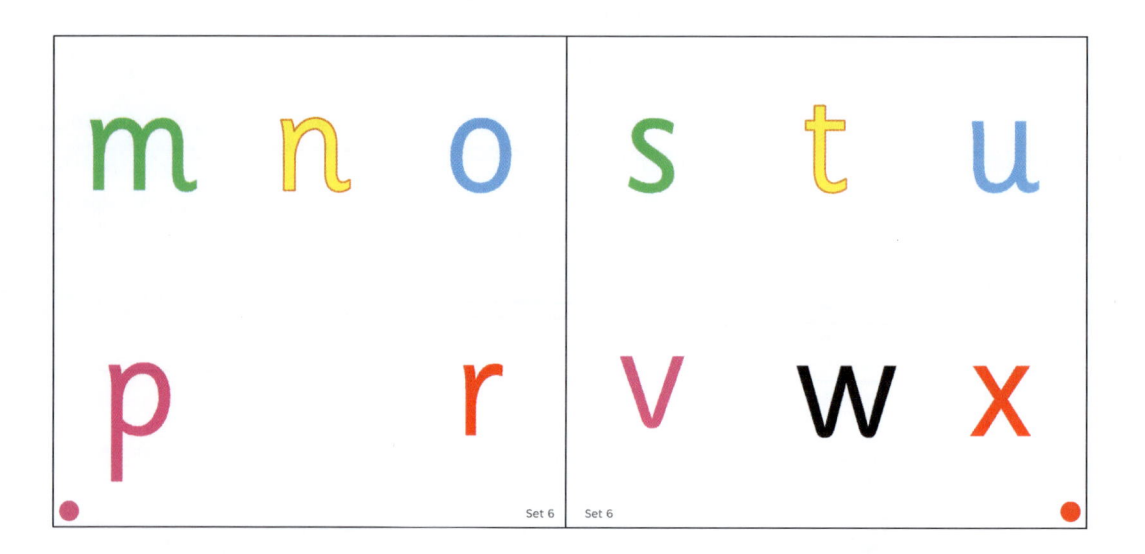

E Tran – Spelling Cards Set 7

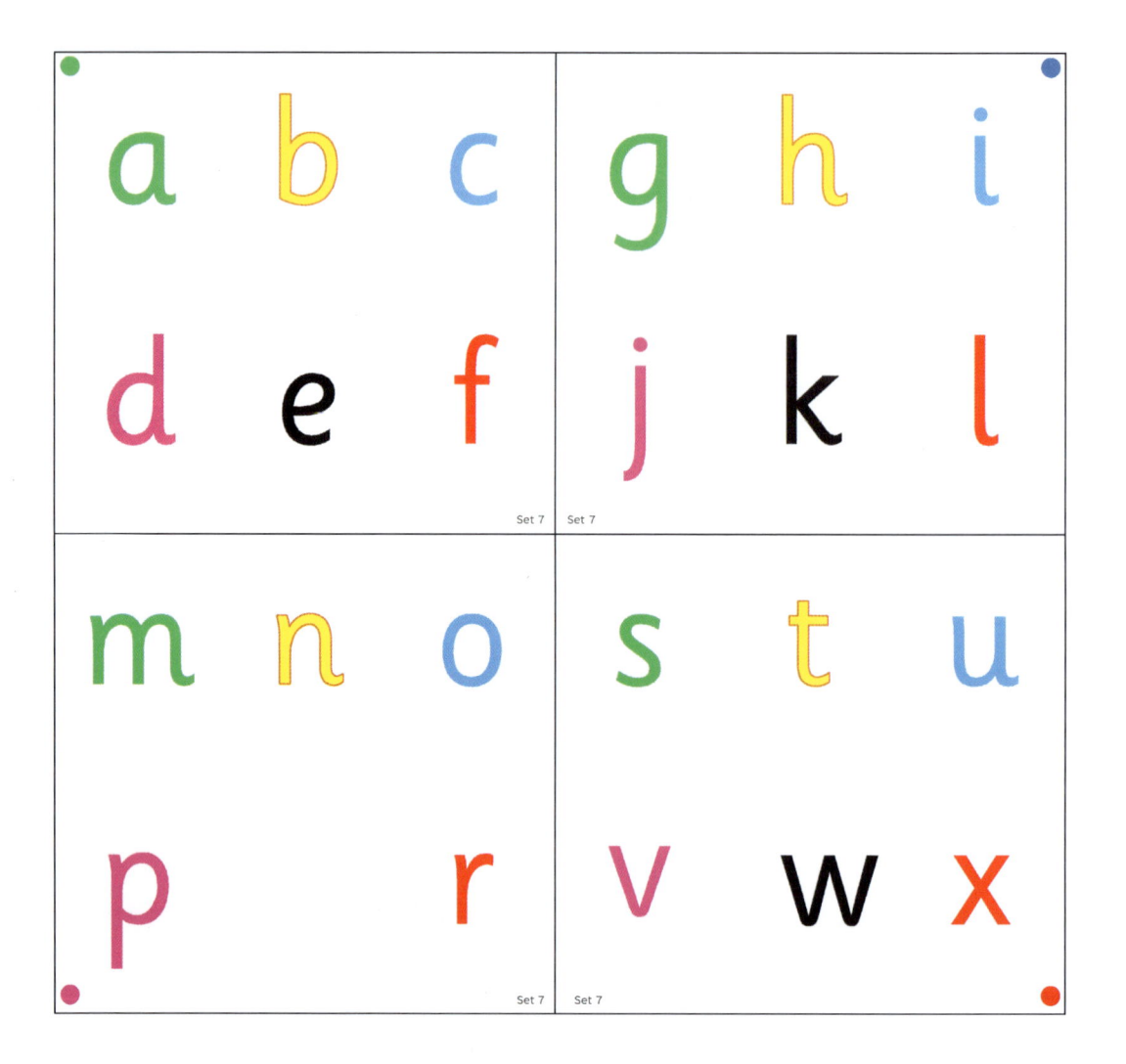

72

y z

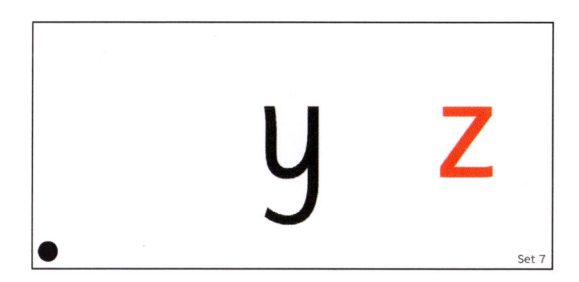

Set 7

E Tran – Spelling Cards (after working on qu in Book 3, use this card at the pink dot)

m n o

p qu r

Bk 3

Movable Alphabet

A comprehensive set of cards with the majority of graphemes of the alphabetic code – print on card and cut out. The cards have a space beneath the grapheme so that the child can push the cards and still see the graphemes.

Refer to the Sound Maps on how the sounds are represented by the graphemes.

s	t	a	p
i	n	m	d
g	o	c	k
e	u	r	h

b	f	l	j
v	w	x	y
z	sh	th	ng
ch	tch	ck	qu
ff	ll	ss	zz

oa	ow	oe	ou
ee	ea	ie	ai
ay	ey	er	ur
ir	or	ar	re
oy	oi	oo	ew

ui	ue	oul	igh
aw	al	au	ore
air	ere	are	ear
our	oar	augh	
eigh	aigh		

ough	e_e
i_e	u_e
a_e	o_e

| ph | gh | le | el |
| il | al | ol | st |

ce	se	sc	ze
bb	bu	dd	ed
wh	pp	wr	rr
rh	ve	ge	gg
gu	nn	mb	kn

| nn | gn | tt | bt |
| xc | cc | ci | ti |

que	cqu
dge	gue
mm	mn

Useful Duplicates

a	e	i	o
u	s	t	p
m	n	d	b

A Place to Read Card
© Ann Sullivan Phonics for SEN 2023

A Place to Read Card
© Ann Sullivan Phonics for SEN 2023

A Place to Read Card
© Ann Sullivan Phonics for SEN 2023

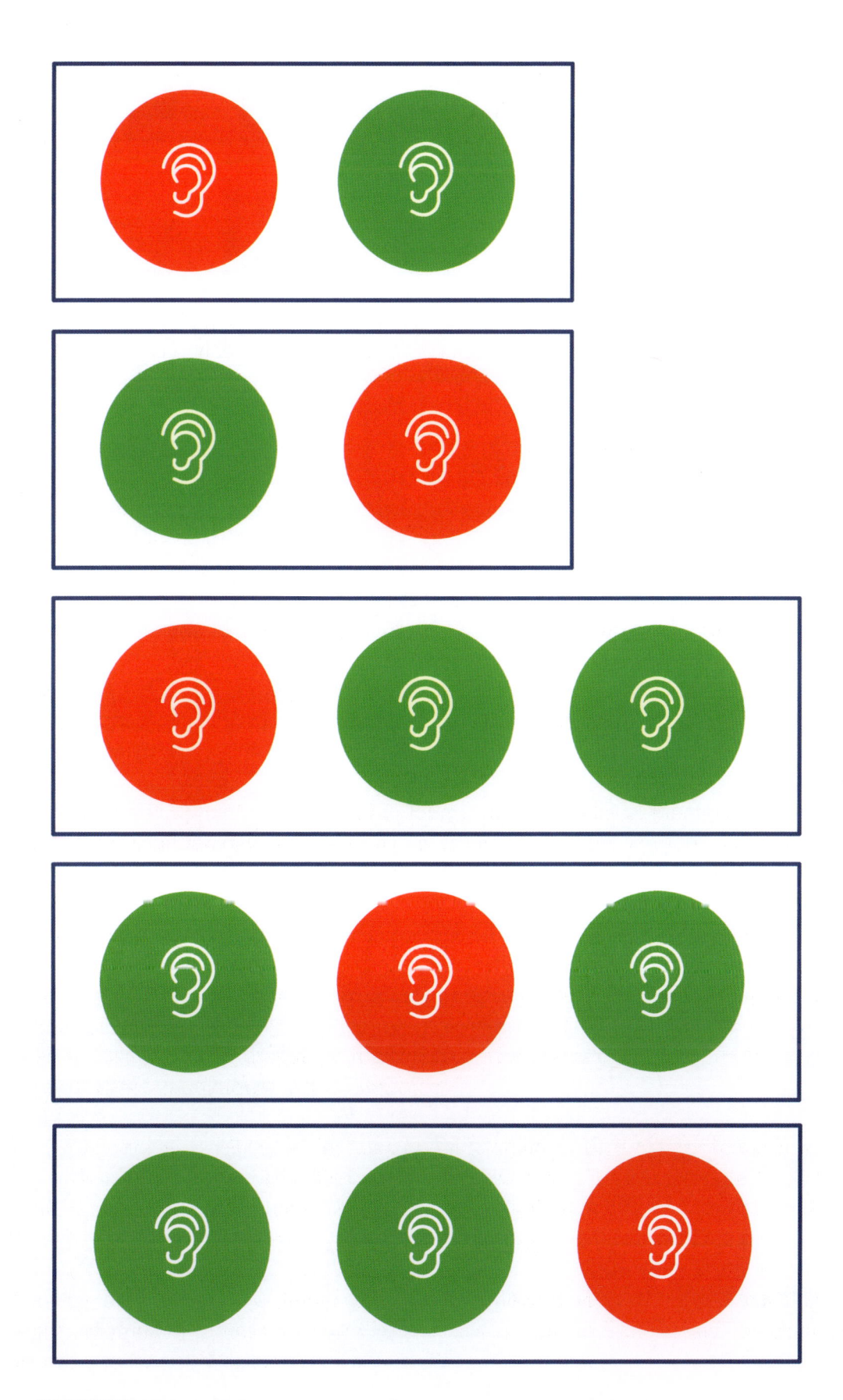

A Place to Listen Cards
© Ann Sullivan Phonics for SEN 2023

Sound Map 1 – variation

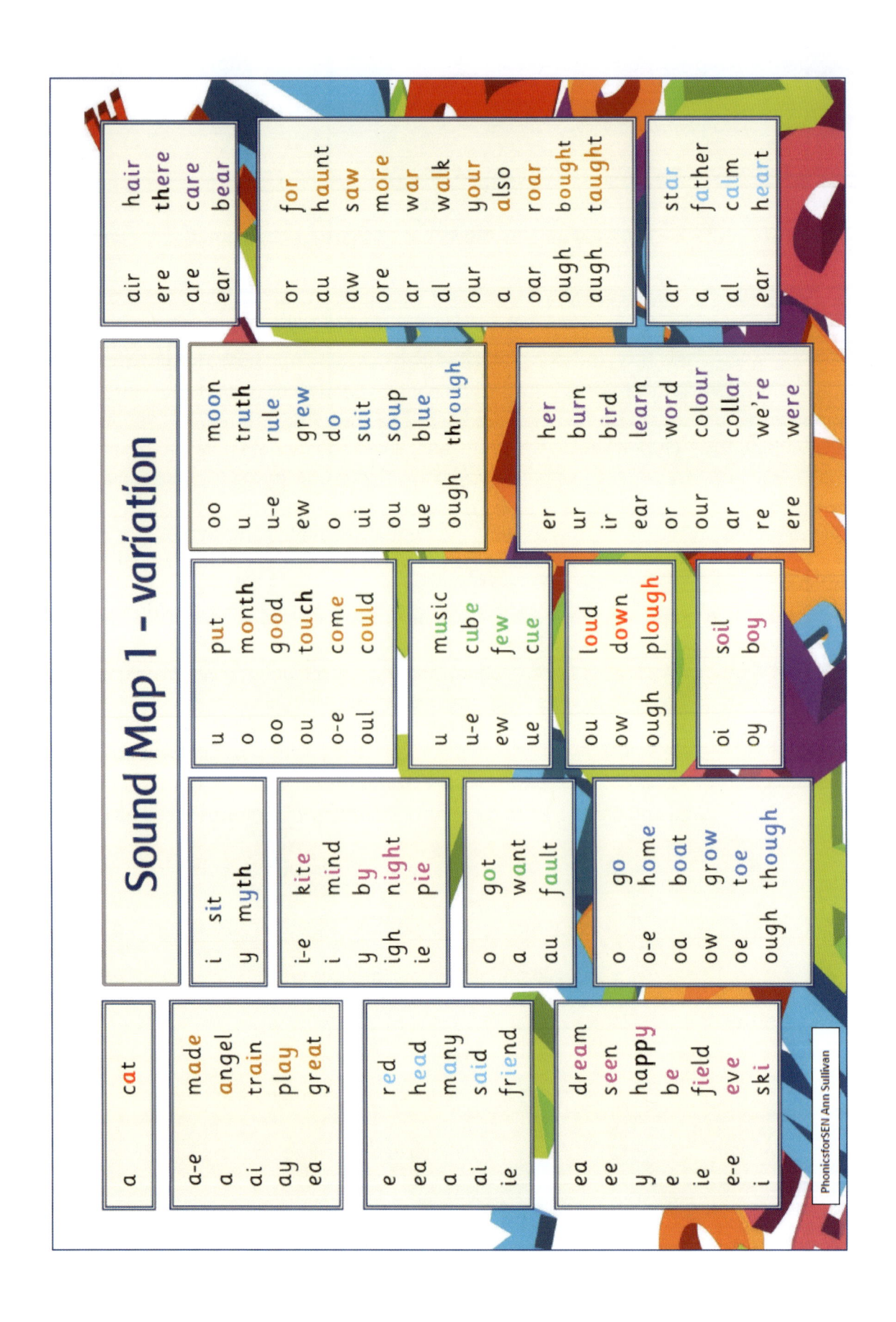

a	cat	

a-e	made
a	angel
ai	train
ay	play
ea	great

i	sit
y	myth

i-e	kite
i	mind
y	by
igh	night
ie	pie

e	red
ea	head
a	many
ai	said
ie	friend

ea	dream
ee	seen
y	happy
e	be
ie	field
e-e	eve
i	ski

air	hair
ere	there
are	care
ear	bear

oo	moon
u	truth
u-e	rule
ew	grew
o	do
ui	suit
ou	soup
ue	blue
ough	through

u	put
o	month
oo	good
ou	touch
o-e	come
oul	could

u	music
u-e	cube
ew	few
ue	cue

o	got
a	want
au	fault

o	go
o-e	home
oa	boat
ow	grow
oe	toe
ough	though

or	for
au	haunt
aw	saw
ore	more
ar	war
al	walk
our	your
a	also
oar	roar
ough	bought
augh	taught

er	her
ur	burn
ir	bird
ear	learn
or	word
our	colour
ar	collar
re	we're
ere	were

ou	loud
ow	down
ough	plough

oi	soil
oy	boy

ar	star
a	father
al	calm
ear	heart

PhonicsforSEN Ann Sullivan

Sound Map 2 - variation

m	man
mm	summer
mn	hymn
mb	lamb

n	not
kn	knot
nn	sunny
gn	gnat

s	treasure
ge	siege
z	azure

t	top
tt	better
bt	doubt

x	fox
xc	except
cc	accept

qu	quick
cqu	acquire

r	rat
wr	wrong
rr	hurry
rh	rhino

v	van
ve	have

j	jam
g	giant
ge	large
dge	bridge

g	get
gg	wiggle
gu	guard
gue	plague
gh	ghost

b	bat
bb	robber
bu	build

y	yes

d	dog
dd	ladder
ed	wagged

w	wig
wh	which

h	hat
wh	whose

p	pet
pp	happy

l	lamp
ll	bell
le	little
el	travel
il	pupil
al	naval
ol	symbol

s	sat
c	city
ss	less
st	listen
ce	dance
se	house
sc	scent

z	zip
s	his
zz	buzz
ze	freeze
se	noise

sh	ship
s	sugar
ch	machine
ci	special
ti	potential

th	think

ch	chip
tch	match

c	can
k	kid
ck	duck
ch	chemist
que	plaque

ng	long

f	fun
ph	phone
ff	stuff
gh	cough

PhonicsforSEN Ann Sullivan

Sound Map 3 - overlap

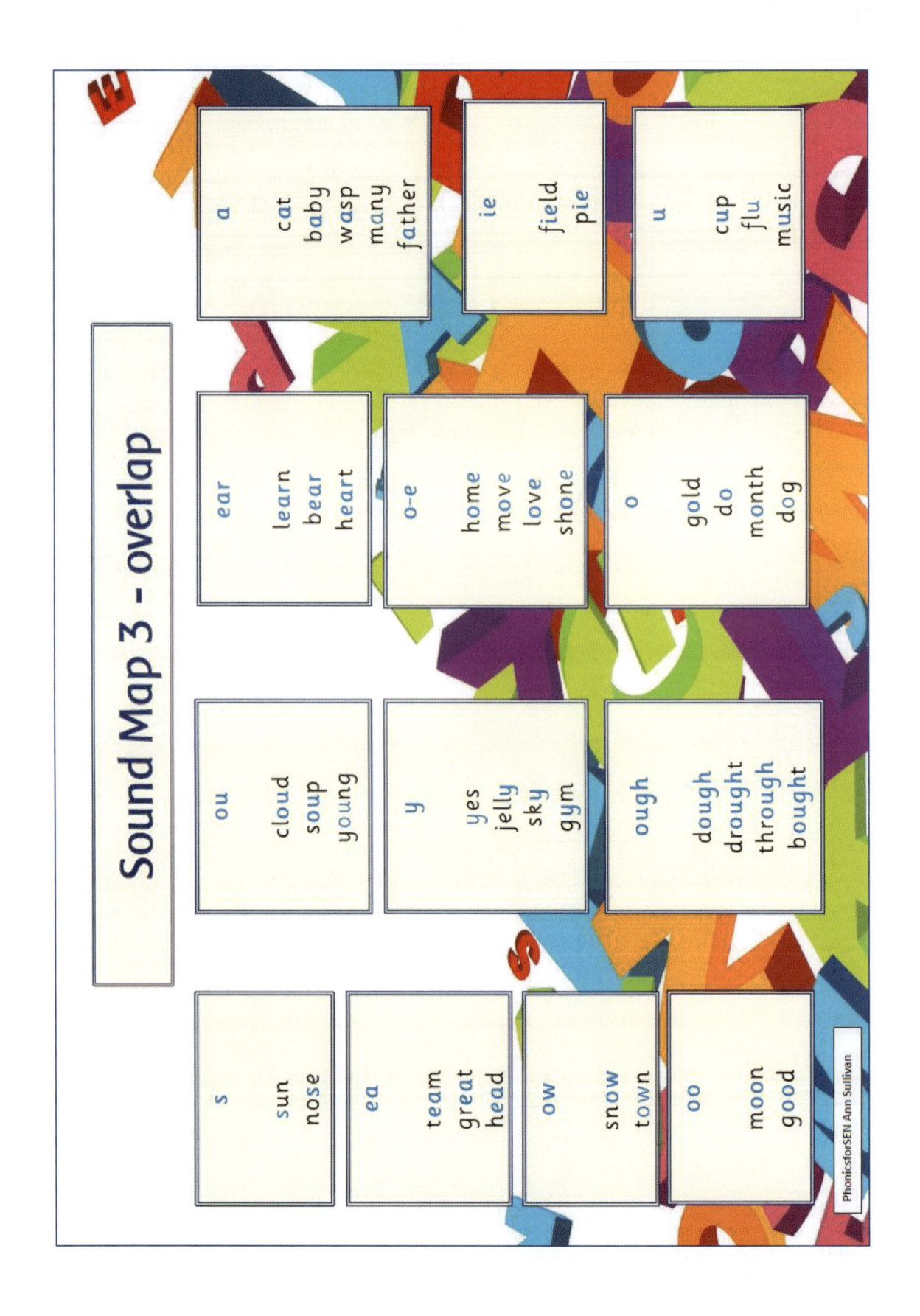

a	ie	u
cat	field	cup
baby	pie	flu
wasp		music
many		
father		

ear	o-e	o
learn	home	gold
bear	move	do
heart	love	month
	shone	dog

ou	y	ough
cloud	yes	dough
soup	jelly	drought
young	sky	through
	gym	bought

s	ea	ow	oo
sun	team	snow	moon
nose	great	town	good
	head		

PhonicsforSEN Ann Sullivan

Glossary

access strategy – a series of planned actions that are used routinely as an alternative presentation to achieve a teaching aim for learners with SEND

accuracy – correctly applying phonic knowledge and skills to successfully decode a printed or written word or encode a spoken word and spell it

adaptation – a change of modification to existing teaching activities, resources or equipment to enable a pupil to access phonics e.g. a pupil uses a movable alphabet to spell a word rather than writing it on a whiteboard

adjustment – alternative provision that enables pupil access in a general sense to the environment and curriculum e.g. a pupil is able to use a tablet and on-screen keyboard to record all writing work across the curriculum

alphabetic code – the relationship between the phonemes in a spoken word and the graphemes in the written word

auditory profile – for pupils with a hearing impairment, an audiogram gives information about their level of deafness and the frequencies of sounds that they can and cannot hear

automaticity – the ability to look at a word and rapidly read it, apparently without any conscious effort – sometimes referred to as reading 'on sight' or 'at a glance'

blending – the ability to 'push' phonemes together or combine them to make a spoken word

decodable reader – a reading book that matches a pupil's knowledge of the alphabetic code at a specific stage in a phonics teaching sequence

decoding – reading a written or printed word – a pupil reads by applying their knowledge of phoneme-grapheme correspondences and phonemic skills

encoding – spelling and writing a spoken word – a pupil spells the word by applying their knowledge of phoneme-grapheme correspondences and phonemic skills

evidence-led – guided by the results and findings of scientific, academic research

fluency – the ability to read with accuracy, automaticity, pace and prosody – the reading sounds like natural speech

formal approach – lessons planned to a timetable, of a defined length, structure and content, led by an instructor

functional literacy – reading, spelling, writing and reading comprehension are at a level that enables a pupil to functionally interact with print in their environment – a general rule of thumb that this is a reading age of 10 years

grapheme – a visual form or figure that is written to represent a phoneme *letter formation* – the act of writing a letter – forming a letter shape using a writing tool

orthographic mapping – a process that happens in the brain when learning to read – it involves the overlaying of the sequence of graphemes on to the sequence of phonemes for a specific word – this information is stored in long-term memory

orthography – the relationship between sounds and letters in terms of common spelling patterns and conventions

overlap – overlap in the alphabetic code relates to the concept that some graphemes can represent more than one phoneme

pace – the ability to read at an appropriate speed without compromising decoding accuracy or understanding

phoneme – the smallest unit of sound in a spoken word

phonemic awareness – the ability to hear, access and manipulate phonemes in spoken words – phonemic awareness is an aspect of phonological awareness

phonics – phonics is not a method – phonics is: 1) a body of knowledge about the alphabetic code (the correspondences between phonemes and graphemes), 2) phonemic and phonological skills and 3) the understanding of some simple concepts about how written language works

phonological awareness – the ability to hear, access and manipulate phonemes and groups of phonemes in spoken language – phoneme, syllable and word level awareness

prosody – the ability to read text so that it sounds like natural speech – includes intonation (change in pitch), rhythm and stress (emphasis given to syllables, key words and phrases)

reading comprehension – the ability to read text and understand it

Scarborough's Reading Rope – a model for reading proposed by Hollis Scarborough - it compares the development of reading competency to the creation of a rope with the elements of reading represented by the fibres and strands of the rope which combine and interact – the two main strands are word recognition and language comprehension

schema – a mental model or framework that helps to organise and interpret information from the world around us

segmenting – the ability to split a spoken word up into its component phonemes in sequence

semi-formal approach – lessons are planned but are delivered in response to a pupil's ability to focus and engage with the teaching and materials at that moment in time

SEND – acronym for Special Educational Needs and Disability in England, otherwise known as additional needs

sensory profile – a description of a pupil's perception and management of sensory stimuli in the environment – the profile outlines varying responses to common stimuli and includes strategies for managing this in the classroom

synthetic phonics – teaching the alphabetic code and phonemic awareness by the synthesis or creation of words from their smallest parts, phonemes and graphemes

systematic phonics – teaching the alphabetic code and phonemic awareness in a highly structured and incremental sequence

The Reading Framework – a document produced by the DfE in July 2021 that outlines best practice in the teaching of reading and spelling – implemented in schools in England

variation - variation in the alphabetic code relates to the concept that some phonemes can be represented by more than one grapheme

visual profile – for pupils with a visual impairment, a visual assessment gives information about their level of vision, their impact on accessing the curriculum and strategies that can be put in place to enable access

whole word reading – reading text by learning words as visual 'whole pictures' without phonic input

word recognition – the ability to read a word either by applying phonics knowledge and skills to decode it or by reading it with automaticity or 'on sight'

About the Phonics for SEN Programme – written by Ann Sullivan

Phonics for Pupils with Special Educational Needs is a systematic and cumulative, synthetic, linguistic phonics (speech to print) programme, with a focus on how sounds are represented by letter(s) in written words (phoneme > grapheme). It has been rigorously designed and developed in the context of peer-reviewed evidence from academic research into all aspects of reading and spelling acquisition. It was published in a series of seven books in 2018 by Speechmark Routledge in the UK and is available from their website and from other online bookshops worldwide.

The programme is divided into seven books as follows:

Book 1: Basic code sounds and letters are introduced in seven groups of sounds or sets with pupils working at the VC and CVC word level.

These are: 1. /s/ /a/ /t/ /p/ 2. /i/ /m/ /n/ /d/ 3. /g/ /o/ /k/ (c k)
4. /e/ /u/ /r/ 5. /h/ /b/ /f/ /l/ 6. /j/ /v/ /w/ x (/k//s/) 7. /y/ /z/

Book 2: No new sounds are introduced but the basic sounds and letters from Book 1 are reinforced, and the word structure is expanded so pupils learn how to read and spell VCC CVCC CCVC and CCVCC words. Book 2 also includes capital letters which can be introduced whenever the teacher feels it is appropriate.

Books 3 – 6: Advanced code sounds are introduced systematically and cumulatively in the following order:
/sh/ /th/ /ng/ /ch/ ck (/k/) qu (/k//w/) tt (/t/) ll (/l/) ss (/s/)
/oa/ /z/ /ee/ /ai/ /er/ /e/ /ou/
/oi/ /oo/ /u/ /ie/ /or/ /air/ /ar/
/s/* /l/* /b/* /d/* (revisited to extend the code) /o/ /i/ /ue/.

In Book 3, the sounds /sh/ and /th/ introduce the pupils to the concept that some sounds are represented by graphemes (sound spellings) that contain more than one letter. From this point on the pupils focus on a single sound at a time and learn all the ways to represent that sound e.g. the sound /ee/ is represented by ee ea e-e y ie e ey, with a focus on the most common sound spellings. As well as studying this variation in the code, the programme also studies the overlap in the code, the concept that some of the sound spellings represent more than one sound e.g. the grapheme 'ea' represents /ee/ in dream, /ai/ in break and /e/ in bread.

Book 7: Syllabification is introduced in book 7, with pupils learning how to read and spell words of 2, 3 and 4 syllables. The main advanced code sounds are also revised but in the context of 2, 3 and 4 syllable words. In the second part of the book pupils work on morphology in the form of suffixes.

The pupils learn, apply and practise knowledge and skills, working at code, word, phrase, sentence and text level throughout the entire programme.

This logical teaching sequence gradually builds up an easy to access 'cognitive map' or schema of how written language is put together and how the sounds are represented in written English, which is great news for pupils with special educational needs.

In addition to this, the programme also includes:
- activities that teach and develop key phonemic skills throughout, i.e. phoneme isolation, dynamic blending, sequential segmenting and phoneme manipulation,
- activities that encourage orthographic mapping (the process that supports the development of a bank of words that pupils can read with automaticity or 'on sight'),
- visual perceptual activities related to the sound spellings, important for pupils with needs in this area.

Additional Resources: Additional resources that supplement the core resources in the books can be found on the Phonics for SEN website. *All of the additional resources are included within the training package that is available.*

Decodable Readers: There are six series of decodable readers that span the Phonics for SEN programme. The books are printed by Discover Inclusion in a simple paper format so that they are affordable for schools. The books are available directly from their website: https://www.discoverinclusion.co.uk/phonics.

Other aspects of the programme

Resource design: The resources and activities in the programme are simple and linear with no unnecessary illustrations or quirky presentations. This conscious design choice aims to limit distraction for SEND pupils and renders the resources age neutral, being appropriate for pupils both young and old.

Language: The programme consciously avoids using technical language with the aim of reducing the cognitive effort and load on pupils. For example, the terms 'sound', 'sound spelling' and 'matching' are used instead of phoneme, grapheme and orthographic mapping.

Development: Phonics for Pupils with SEN has been developed over 20 years or so. It is led by the evidence of academic research into how children learn to read, commonly referred to as 'the science of reading'. It has been used successfully with many students with complex SEND including ASD, MLD, SLD, SLCN (including pupils who are preverbal or nonverbal) and those who have significant physical disabilities. It is primarily used as an intervention in mainstream schools and as a programme for initial instruction in specialist schools. Phonics for SEN fulfils the requirements of the Reading Framework – Teaching the Foundations of Literacy DfE 2021.

Assessment and Progress Tracking: Paper based assessment materials are available from Phonics for SEN. The programme is also now supported on the Phonics Tracker online tool and on B Squared.

Using the Programme: All of the books contain a comprehensive 'Working through the Programme' section which explains the theory and rationale of the programme as well as how each activity is to be carried out. This is written to be accessible for all adults teaching reading and spelling. To further support those delivering the programme, there are instructions and prompts at the top of every worksheet or task page.

Training for Schools: Flexible and sustainable training for schools is available in the form of a course that covers all aspects of phonics and how to deliver the Phonics for Pupils with SEN programme.

Phonics for Pupils with SEN website:
https://www.phonicsforpupilswithspecialeducationalneeds.com/

Printed in Great Britain
by Amazon